Ground Stop

Ground Stop

✦

An Inside Look at the Federal Aviation Administration on September 11, 2001

Pamela S. Freni

iUniverse, Inc.

New York Lincoln Shanghai

Ground Stop
An Inside Look at the Federal Aviation Administration on September 11, 2001

iUniverse, Inc.

For information address:
iUniverse, Inc.
2021 Pine Lake Road, Suite 100
Lincoln, NE 68512
www.iuniverse.com

ISBN: 0-595-29738-2

Printed in the United States of America

This book is dedicated to everyone who works for the Federal Aviation Administration; may they never have to experience another 9/11, but if they do, may they manage the next one as brilliantly as they did the first.

"These are the times in which a genius would wish to live. It is not in the still calm of life, or the repose of a pacific station, that great characters are formed. The habits of a vigorous mind are formed in contending with difficulties. Great necessities call out great virtues. When a mind is raised, and animated by scenes that engage the heart, that those qualities which would otherwise lay dormant, wake into life and form the character of the hero and the statesman."

—Abigail Adams in a letter to her son John Quincy Adams

Contents

Acknowledgements

There are a number of people to whom I owe an enormous debt of gratitude for helping me create this book. To a large extent, they are the thousands of nameless people who were manning their posts on 9/11, the majority continue to do so. They are all very dedicated and special people.

Special thanks go to all those who took the time to speak with me and help me understand the exotic world of air-traffic control, management, investigations, and a myriad of other special tasks that are accomplished each day by the Federal Aviation Administration (FAA). They include Bill Peacock, Director of Air Traffic Service (AAT-1), Sabra Kaulia, Division Manager for Air Traffic Airspace Management (ATA-1), Linda Schuessler (ATT-100), Tony Ferrante, Manager of Air Traffic Investigations (AAT-200), Tony Mello, Assistant Manager of Air Traffic Investigations (AAT-201), Mike Cirillo (ATP-1), Kevin Kiss, controller at Ft. Worth Air Route Traffic Control Center, Dave Lubore, commercial pilot, Luis Ramirez, manager of air traffic operations for the Washington Air Route Traffic Control Center, Dave Canoles, Manager of Evaluations and Investigations Staff (AAT-20), Larry Bicknell, retired FAA manager of Washington, D.C. Reagan National Airport, Frank Hatfield, then air traffic manager of Eastern Region (AEA-500), Rick Hostetler, member of Planning and Procedures Program Special Operations Division, Jack Kies, Air Traffic Tactical Operations (ATT-1), Gregg Dvorak, manager of the FAA's Operational Support Program (AOS-1), Debbie Herbert, Susan Ball, and Cathy and Ed Kelly, retired Deputy Director of Airway Facilities Service (AAF-2). And a thousand thanks to the most intrepid of all people who soldiers on with only words as his weapon, Jerry Lavey, internal communications director for the FAA administrator (AOA-3). His support, encouragement, and continual watchfulness opened many doors for me that would have otherwise escaped my notice.

Photo Descriptions

Page 10—Airway Traffic Control Station at Newark, N.J. in 1936; precursor to the first air route traffic control centers (ARTCC). (courtesy of FAA)

Page 24—First air traffic controller, Archie W. League with flags in winter at St. Louis, Missouri. (courtesy of FAA)

Page 25—Airport Surveillance Radar (ASR-1) from 1950s. (courtesy of FAA)

Page 28—Dulles International Airport construction. (courtesy of FAA)

Page 34—FAA headquarters building in Washington, D.C. (courtesy of FAA)

Page 62—Traffic display showing airborne airplanes at 8:47am as AA11 strikes the north tower of the World Trade Center. (courtesy of FAA)

Page 68—Traffic display showing remaining airborne airplanes at 11:06am; system is closed until further notice. (courtesy of FAA)

Page 83—President Franklin Roosevelt laying corner stone at Washington Reagan National Airport in Washington, D.C. in 1940. (courtesy of FAA)

Page 94—Air traffic control tower at Atlanta's Hartsfield International Airport with flag during the week after September 11, 2001. (courtesy of Susan Ball)

1

Working for the federal government today is emotionally difficult at best. Traditionally, politics has always included excoriation of government workers as standard stump fare. Many a President has ridden into office on the backs of the federal workers vowing at every whistle stop to put large numbers of them on the streets in an effort to cut federal spending.

Federal workers have been sneeringly called "bureaucrats," "members of a bloated system," or other equally pejorative terms, yet shortly after 8:45am on September 11, 2001, many of these bureaucrats came to the rescue of the nation in the form of policemen, firemen, air-traffic controllers, lawyers, sailors, fighter pilots, National Guard members, and emergency management personnel. Members of the organizations represented by these people—the Federal Aviation Administration (FAA), Federal Emergency Management Administration (FEMA), NORAD, Department of Justice, and the Coast Guard—would not sleep for days as they valiantly strove to mitigate the damage done by nineteen terrorists who hijacked four airplanes and used them as cruise missiles, destroying the World Trade Towers in New York City, seriously damaging the Pentagon near Washington, DC, and crashing the fourth plane into a lonely field in southern Pennsylvania. As they struggled to reassert control over the country and in turn stabilize the aviation industry and the air-traffic control system, the actions of many of these government workers undoubtedly saved the lives of others.

Renowned *Washington Post* editorialist David S. Broder noted in the subsequent weeks, "Whatever their views before Sept. 11, Americans of all stripes have relearned the lesson that when there is a crisis, it's handy to have a government that can cope." [1] Not only cope, but also race to the rescue of those in need the most.

Stephen Barr, Federal Diary writer for the *Washington Post*, agreed. He penned in his column a few days after the tragedy, "When disaster strikes, everyone expects public servants to swing into action." He listed all the actions the nation expects to be taken, in order to mend it in times of disaster—rescue, communication, and transportation—emphasizing the simplicity of the list, yet acknowledging that the job isn't ever easy. Barr said in times of crisis that all eyes are on government workers, wanting them to show the country the way back to sanity. He quotes former counsel to the Senate Governmental Affairs Committee Steven L. Katz who says about federal workers, that they "…recognize that 'it is now their job to rally to strengthen the nation.' The efforts we will see from federal workers will be a personal best to benefit the nation." [2]

In a personal best for many government workers, as the terrorist attacks unfolded, the FAA declared, in a hitherto unexercised action, a national ground stop, requiring all airplanes on the ground to stay there and any in the air to land immediately at the nearest airport. The quick and potentially career-ending call to ground all planes by FAA middle managers undoubtedly saved lives, trapping nascent hijacking schemes before they could fully fledge into deadly, pyrotechnic disasters in other cities. With around five thousand commercial flights in the air, the "land-immediately" order caused a huge traffic jam of airplanes for which air traffic controllers suddenly became responsible for untangling while also making sure none of the airplanes bumped into one another. Other FAA personnel hunkered down, manning the emergency response system, working out the kinks in the security processes while trying to determine how to return the system to normal from its newly-induced state of slumber.

On September 11, as danger loomed, almost everyone in Washington, D.C. evacuated the area—everyone that is except for hundreds of bureaucrats considered critical personnel. They simply continued working during the crisis, oblivious to threats to their safety. Others, not designated as critical, volunteered in the emergency response areas, forgoing the chance to leave the city, potentially under attack by other terrorists, and helped where they could. They stayed, going home for a couple hours of sleep, returning, enduring another twenty hours of crisis management. So many volunteered in the days to come that some had to be turned away.

As the nation reacted to the civil servants' sacrifices, David Kerr, spokesman for the FAA's Research and Acquisition organization, wrote in a weekly newsletter, "It's something I wasn't sure I would ever see. I have never worked for the Government at a time when, well, we in the Civil Service were all that popular with the public. The last twenty years have mostly been sort of a test between politicians to see which one was going to do more to reel in the Federal Government." He continued, "But things seem to have changed. After September 11th, one of the grimmest experiences we have ever faced as a nation, the public seems to have revised their opinion of government and in particular the civil service." [3]

Paul C. Light, Brookings Institute director of governmental studies recently compiled a list of achievements accomplished by our government including, "rebuilding Europe after World War II, establishing the interstate highway system, sending men to the moon, and curing horrible diseases." [4] We as a nation seem to make all of these mountainous tasks easy, but choose not to publicize them as true wonders of the world. The dedication of the people in successfully creating any one of these actions and many, many more just like them should be applauded by the nation, but only at times of crisis are the civil servants finally recognized as the dedicated warriors they are. Thousands of engineers, analysts, lawyers, administrative personnel, architects, and law-enforcement officers in the government labor in obscurity until a crisis hits. Only then does the nation recognize their worth as a quality work force, critical in the continuity of the nation's business. It's unfortunate, but we may truly be at our best when things are at their worst. This is the story of one of those times.

2

September 21, 2001—There was laughter on the streets of Washington, D.C. today. For the first time in ten days people felt safe enough to stand on the street corners in glorious weather in groups of three and four, talking and laughing as some of the gripping strain from the recently harrowing events slowly and surely melted from their faces. Present still was an underlying tension as people tried to fit into the new skin given them by horrendous terrorists' acts ten days before. Their world had changed in a second from one of relative safety to one of twisted terror that they hardly recognized. Until now, numerous generations had been born and raised with relatively minimal threat—the childlike trust that American borders and vast oceans were rock solid in the face of world hate had made the contemplation of fictional breaches seem like fun. Now, everyone knew the truth.

The evening before, spirits had been buoyed tremendously by a magnificent speech given by President George W. Bush. This, plus the passage of time, was giving everyone a tiny sense of perspective as it widened the gulf from the moment "it" happened until now. President Bush's declaration gave heart and substance to the American people's feelings when he said: "Our grief has turned to anger and anger to resolution." And he gave the populace a sense of determination when he continued, "Whether we bring our enemies to justice or bring justice to our enemies, justice will be done." [1]

On the evening of September 21, people took refuge in major league baseball games, restarted throughout the nation as a return to "normal" was attempted. One game was played near Washington, D.C. between the Baltimore Orioles and the New York Yankees at Camden Yards in Baltimore, Maryland. The evening had months ago been billed as the beginning of the final home stand of Baltimore's favorite son Cal Ripken, but since terrorists had destroyed the World Trade Center Towers and damaged the Pentagon on September 11, no one had had the time to think about the end of a glorious career. The country had to think about starting over with a new set of rules.

That night, before the game began, the Baltimore Fire Department stationed personnel at every entrance of the ballpark. They used buckets to collect money for the charity fund supporting the New York City firemen who had on September 11 taken a large part of the burden of the New York City attacks. Over three hundred of them were killed in the collapse of the Twin Towers. Grim, but necessary, the Baltimore units seemed happy to have something to do and the 47,099 people in attendance donated over $22,000 as they filed through the brick promenade, entering the ball field.

People were reaching out to one another. Two men, strangers, in their late forties, spotted each other in the crowd and by virtue of their clothing (a billed cap with fire company insignia on it and a tee shirt with another fire company insignia) recognized that destiny had given them a common profession. As they approached each other, obviously glad to see a kindred spirit in light of the huge losses of New York City firemen, one asked the other if he minded a hug. The crowd filed past the two, leaving them entwined in a manly embrace, strangers no longer. Common professions were complemented by a common need of the human spirit.

As thousands of people filed into the baseball stadium, the clock ticked away the minutes before the start of the game. As the clock on the scoreboard ticked from 7:04:59 to 7:05, a local fire company began posting the colors to the middle of center field. The crowd came to its feet as a large door in the corner of right field slid open and men and women in blue and white uniforms filed out toward home plate. They walked the right field foul line until reaching home plate and turned up the left field foul line, filling all the spaces from home to each base, first and third. The announcer told the audience that these were members of many of the local fire and rescue companies who had been first responders at the Pentagon when it had been attacked. They had rushed to the Pentagon from Arlington County, Montgomery County, and Fairfax County. Others had responded from the Maryland and Virginia state search-and-rescue teams and were now taking time out to accept a salute from their fellow Americans.

A huge American flag slowly and elegantly unfurled down the red brick wall of the east side of the Yard. The crowd, already on its feet cheering, became even louder. The dugout emptied as the players stepped up to the lines and intermingled with the blue uniforms of the emergency personnel—the right line of blue intertwined with the black, white, and orange of the Orioles' uniforms, the left line mingling with the gray and blue of the Yankees' uniforms. Large American flags on poles appeared at the end of each line nearest the bases—Orioles hero Cal Ripken holding one and New York Yankees great Roger Clemmons the other. They served as exclamation points to the statement being made by the men and women standing between the bases and home plate: the inhabitants of the United States represent a proud and free nation, one that values its people over all else.

A moment of silence was announced. Baseball crowds are not known for their stillness, and even though tens of thousands were packed into the ball field, it was as though the pennants hanging above the walls were holding their breath. As the silence drew to a close, no one stirred as a member of the U.S. Navy played *Taps*, a single horn in a lonely and time-honored ritual assigning the country's dead into God's hands. A woman with a brilliant voice sang the national anthem. Her voice was strong and clear, savoring each nuance of the melody, giving each word added meaning.

Anyone who performs the *Star Spangled Banner* in Camden Yards for the first time is usually startled as the crowd *ad libs* a loud "Oh!" at the beginning of the second stanza of the anthem. It's a tradition as a word play on the nickname for the Orioles. For the first time in recent memory no one defamed the song—now a precious talisman to each person. Not a single "Oh!" was uttered.

The rescuers filed from the field and the Orioles and the Yankees lined up, end-of-game style, shaking hands with every one of them before the first responders were allowed to march away. The crowd was on its feet cheering madly until all were out of sight—"USA!" "USA!" "USA!" Only two weeks before, the world had been a very different place.

3

September 10, 2001—The air-traffic system of the United States supported and guided 35,000 commercial flights to their destinations without a single notable problem. As a tiny slice of the millions of planes that are directed each year through the air-traffic control system of the United States flew across the country, each one took off and landed without any significant incidents. September 10 was a Monday—the preferred day of travel for business flyers, leaving those flying on Tuesday, Wednesday, and Thursday a little more leg room. Tuesdays are normally light travel days on the airplanes. Fridays are impossibly crowded because everyone always hurries to return home at the end of the week.

FAA manager Tony Ferrante was one of those Monday travelers as he left Washington, D.C., and flew to Chicago on September 10. Ferrante, the manager of the FAA's air-traffic investigation arm, was traveling to Chicago to testify on the FAA's behalf at a hearing on Tuesday. Another Monday traveler was Gregg Dvorak, manager of the FAA's Operational Support Program, who was traveling to Nashua, New Hampshire, to give a lecture.

September 11, 2001—Dawn broke on a beautiful day on the East Coast. Federal Aviation Administration Eastern Region Air Traffic manager Frank Hatfield called it "drop-dead gorgeous." The sunlight glowing in the morning had over the last few weeks shifted from overhead to slightly further south, a harbinger of the changing seasons. It was a day for glorying in the beauty and clarity of the season. The vernal equinox was less than two weeks away, bringing fall, always a much-welcomed time of year to the eastern seaboard. As summer waned, the quality of the light changed from directly overhead to indirect, lighting the world in a different way, with temperatures moderating. Most who reside in the New England and mid-Atlantic environs during this autumnal period are envied by the rest of the nation, proven by the thousands of tourists who stream into the area for a peek at the season's blazing foliage.

Ignoring all of this, passengers hurried toward Boston's Logan Airport, trying to catch American Airlines flight 11 (AA11). Destined for Los Angeles, it was scheduled to leave the ground at 8:00am. Some had been scheduled to travel on this flight. Others had changed their plans and were unexpectedly flying on this airplane. Getting to Logan proved to be a little tricky because of all the construction at the entrance of the tunnel leading to the airport. The Big Dig, as it is called, required traffic detours to get to the passageway leading to the airport complex. Then there was the time it took for parking and of course checking in. But, despite all the roadblocks, ninety-two made it to the airplane before the doors closed.

Finally, AA11 lumbered down the runway at 7:59am, on time, taking off into the azure blue. Air traffic controllers from Logan's control tower sent the big airplane on its way with a communications handoff to the next way station. As the plane gained altitude, the Boston Air Route Traffic Control Center (ARTCC) took control of the flight in a handoff from the Boston Terminal Radar Approach Control (TRACON), giving it clearance to fly across an imaginary air-traffic map in the sky toward Cleveland. The controller at the Boston ARTCC gave the airliner the okay to climb to 29,000 feet. As the plane reached the intermediate altitude, the air traffic controller said, "American, you are cleared to climb to 31,000." [1]

Air-traffic control in the United States, as with all other countries, is an incredibly complex process complete with controllers, very specific rules of engagement, and complicated equipment responsible for the safe journeys of millions of flights a year. Air traffic is managed by moving airplanes to their destinations with the use of narrow pathways throughout the country centered on ground-based navigation aids. Planes fly, responding to controller instructions, to a navigation aid, then turn toward another until they have tacked to their destination. Speed and altitude vary, creating a stacking effect so that as many airplanes as possible can be fit into the airspace. The intricate process results in juggling over 35,000 airplanes through a limited amount of airspace every twenty-four hours, every day of the year, with every one of the 18,000 FAA's air-traffic controllers playing a small but critical part of the process.

The term air traffic control is actually a misnomer. Despite what the words say, most planes are monitored long before they ever leave the ground and streak into the air. Each day as the sun rises, waves of scheduled commercial, passenger-bearing flights rise up from the east and spend hours flying west. Every flight requires positive control throughout its journey by the people located in remote facilities scattered around the country. Beginning at the moment a plane traveling under instrument flight rule (IFR) conditions—positive management of an aircraft based on a flight plan—leaves the gate and heads for a runway at most airports it is under management of a controller located in the tower. Each person works a position specifically tailored for a particular action occurring at the airport—taxiing, inbound flights, and outbound flights—with each plane being moved around the asphalt or atmospheric dance floor with precision bred of each person, controller and pilot, knowing exactly what to do at each turn.

Controllers in the tower at each airport handle ground traffic (airplanes with wheels still touching the asphalt) and local traffic (airplanes flying very near the airport), making busy airports a constantly changing canvas of radar blips. The first instructions to a departing airplane come from the ground control position in the tower. As taxiing instructions are completed and the plane queued for take-off, the local control position takes over. The dance continues, from the local position to the next phase for aircraft take off, as another controller takes command—those managing the airspace of multiple airports. These TRACON personnel are responsible for disentangling the swirling traffic as it enters or leaves the airspace from several airports such as the four in Washington, D.C.—Dulles International, Reagan National Airport, Baltimore-Washington Airport, and Andrews Air Force Base.

As the air traffic rises around Washington, the TRACON controllers manage the flow into a pre-set pattern with invisible sky lanes. They provide instructions including heading, altitude, and frequency information for contacting the ARTCC—the high-altitude, en route air managers in the United States—at one of twenty-one regional air route traffic control centers. The ARTCC controller takes over at the edge of the terminal airspace—about fifty miles from the airport. The en route controllers at the ARTCCs move the traffic around at cruising altitudes, handing each flight off as it moves from one region to another—New York City to Washington, or Washington to Atlanta or Cleveland, for instance. Throughout the entire progression, positive control is the defining factor of safety, with separation—vertically and horizontally—the controllers' constant watchword.

The buildings housing the en route operations are giant pulsing centers of activity, twenty-four hours a day, seven days a week. Many have been in existence for more than seventy years, having begun their stint as privately owned operations. In the beginning the purely low-tech operation was born from industry need, with a consortium of airlines organizing and furnishing personnel to run the first airway traffic control center at Newark, New Jersey on December 1, 1935. Two others soon followed—Chicago in April 1936 and Cleveland in June 1936. In 1936, as the aviation industry was recognized as a national interest, these operations were converted to federal control. Fifteen employees made up the original cadre. The Boston ARTCC, the building from which AA11 was being overseen, was the fifteenth center to be opened. It was commissioned on December 7, 1941.

A minimum of two years of professional training in the FAA's education system is required just to get a chance to control traffic. In order to earn a job at one of the major control facilities one needs years of experience and an exhibition of true skill. Gaining a spot controlling at one of the en route facilities takes from three to five years—a combination of formal and on-the-job training. Once there, controllers gladly face each day of moving planes from one point in the airspace to another, mumbling incantations known only to them and the pilots into communications links that beam them into the sky where they are caught by an airplane that responds to their every wish.

Air traffic manager at the New York ARTCC, Mike McCormick, had gone through these steps on his way through his career. Within days of the controllers' strike in August 1981, he signed up for the rigorous training and became a controller, moving through many positions until landing the top job at the New York facility. He had controlled at Philadelphia tower, worked in the Eastern Region office, been the assistant air-traffic manager at the New York TRACON, then the deputy at the Washington ARTCC, before winding up at the New York ARTCC. He loved every job, but this one was the reason he had signed up twenty years ago. Here he was able to make a difference—currently he was working on lowering the operational error rate. It was at a ten-year low. On September 11, he was expecting a quiet day of strategic planning.

Flight AA11, cleared for 31,000 feet, was under the direction of a controller at the Boston ARTCC. By now passengers on the plane had settled in, relaxing with their headsets on or their laptops opened on the tray tables at their seats. At 8:14am, another plane, United Airlines flight 175 (UA175), also bound for Los Angeles, left Logan Airport. They too were handed off to the Boston ARTCC and given permission to climb to cruising altitude. As UA175 left the ground, flight AA11 quit responding to the controller's communications. It failed to climb toward cruising altitude. The Boston ARTCC controller called: "American, this is Boston Center. How do you read?" [2] He continued calling. After repeating the words twelve times, he asked other controllers in the facility to call AA11 on other frequencies. Receiving no response from the flight deck, they thought that maybe the plane had experienced a radio failure—maybe the airplane couldn't communicate with anyone, yet was still flying in its original direction. As the communications blackout in AA11 continued the controllers began vectoring other airplanes out of its path, to avoid a midair collision. UA175 was one of several planes moved away from the assumed path of the missing flight. It, like others, was repositioned on a path that would take it away from the first plane.

Then as controllers watched, AA11 disappeared from the radar. Something or someone on the plane had caused the transponder to malfunction. Normally, this electronic signal is tuned to a specific code that corresponds (squawks) to computer information indicating the air carrier and flight identification number, speed, and altitude, which in turn displays this identifying flight information on the controller screen. Nothing flashed on the screen where only seconds ago the controller had seen the plane.

The en route controller asked other planes in the air to try to contact the errant flight. UA175 was one of the flights asked to try to raise AA11. No one was able to get any response from the American flight. Problems with communications equipment are not too unusual and sometimes different equipment, frequencies, or locales can bridge the problem between an aircraft and air-traffic control. Even with the help of others, no response came from Captain Jim Ogonowski or copilot Tom McGuinness on AA11.

Unbeknownst to the controllers, the only communication from AA11 was through a jury-rigged hookup from a flight attendant, Betty Ong, who was speaking through a reservations agent in North Carolina to the American Airlines' operations center. Ong reported a grim picture on the plane—a passenger dead and a crewmember wounded. As Ong described the vicious personal attacks and the controllers feverishly worked on re-establishing contact with the first plane, a second, UA175, also quit responding.

Air-traffic control is like a daily, exotic dance carried out at three different levels all over the United States. When a commercial aircraft readies to leave on a flight, the dance begins. Every move and action is choreographed from push back away from the terminal building at its originating airport until rolling up to the jet way at its destination. Each *pas de deux* is danced with a different partner—one while the aircraft is on the ground and in the terminal proximity, one at mid-level altitudes, and one when the plane finally reaches high altitudes. So to have two airplanes incommunicado at the same time in the same proximity was worrisome to the controller—left by himself, dancing blind and without a partner. This could mean many things, but one of those was chilling—hijack.

Hijackings were rare in the world until about 1947 when they became popular as a method for fleeing Eastern bloc countries after communism shut down free passage from the East into Western Europe. In subsequent years, Cuban citizens used hijacking airplanes as a favorite method of letting their feet do the talking as they exited a country with no future. Oddly enough, in the 1960s hijackings began to flow the other way—U.S. to Cuba. The first one of this type occurred on May 1, 1961 as a plane scheduled to land in Key West, Florida, was forced to go to Cuba. As hijacking became epidemic, a method of behavioral profiling was established to help determine potentially suspicious passengers and make sure they were never allowed to board aircraft. This, added to increasingly sophisticated weapon-detection technology, has lowered the hijacking rates in America to almost nil.

Bill Peacock, FAA Director of Air Traffic Services, was readying for a meeting in New Orleans with the National Air Traffic Controllers Association (NATCA), the controllers' union, on September 11, to see if their dance could be done with fewer or tighter steps. The FAA has an enormous number of constituencies to satisfy including each of several unions, contractors, commercial airlines, airports, and the military. Peacock was intent on working that day with the largest union. His beeper chimed at just after 8:00am EST. His staff was calling to alert him of a possible hijack. When AA11 failed to respond to communications, the FAA headquarters in Washington was notified.

It was normal procedure for the information to be relayed to Peacock—among many other duties, he is the ultimate manager of all the air-traffic controllers in the country's system. A thirty-year veteran, he is tall and slender, with an air of command about him. Peacock is a quiet man with a smoothness in expressing himself that comes from many years as a controller—speaking for hours a day, in sometimes tense situations.

A victim of its own success, by 2001 the aviation system in the U.S. had become increasingly moribund—flights late or cancelled and delays mounting to an economically unacceptable level. In response to this system overload, Peacock had spent most of 2001 trying to fix the problem by wringing out any additional efficiencies from the part of the system over which he had jurisdiction—the controlling process. Much of the delay problems lay in areas over which he had no power—runway capacity at airports, weather and weather prediction capability, and scheduling overload by the airlines. But if his organization could help in any way, his job was to figure out how, which was the reason for his being in Louisiana on Tuesday.

Daily, Peacock pondered the variables in the process used to move airplanes from one location to another. Significant numbers of new runways needed to land more airplanes were years away. At a cost of billions of dollars each, airports were reluctant to pay for additional concrete except as a last resort. Weather was always an unpredictable factor and the air-traffic manager knew that the FAA was working on several predictive tools, all months and years away as well. The third factor in the mix was the airlines all wanting to land and takeoff from major airports at the same time. Each commercial company had schedules chock full of takeoffs supposed to depart the most popular airports from 7:00am until 9:00am and landings from 3:00pm until 7:00pm. All of them could not possibly fit into the schedule—yet they continued to blame the FAA when timetables were missed. With these three problems seemingly un-manageable, Peacock worked on the one part of the puzzle he could control.

As had been typical, the week of September 4 was crowded with meetings and discussions involving capacity-driven delays. Worries centered on analysis of August's numbers indicating delays were rising, obviously not what FAA administrator, Jane Garvey, had wanted to hear. Peacock concentrated on any means that could be used in reducing and eliminating the rising trend of late departures and arrivals. As part of the process, the controllers' union was included in the mix. In a perfect world, air traffic could possibly be controlled exclusively by computers, but in an imperfect world of wind, weather, equipment, and human factors the controllers are the adaptation link that manipulates and manages 35,000 flights a day using very well-established rules to do a minuet in the sky of ever-changing factors. The meeting in New Orleans was to determine if a safe way existed of using technology to gain ground on some of the capacity issues. Now, Peacock was being informed of a possible hijacking in progress.

Hijack suspicions rarely pan out in this day and age of the magnetometer screenings of passengers at airports. It's very difficult for conventional weaponry to be smuggled past airport checkpoints and onto airplanes, so hijackings in the United States are relatively rare. At this point, the controllers had only suspicions and had reported them just in case. Peacock waited for the next call. His experience had taught him that hijackers generally made demands for something—either a place to land or safe transit to a particular location. His job was to determine if the hijacking was real, then to alert proper authorities—usually the FBI. When the plane landed safely, his job was over and the issue became a law enforcement one.

Peacock didn't know it yet, but on this day in September, the hijacking rate in the U.S. had suddenly skyrocketed. The second airplane to disappear from the controller's scope, UA175, with its load of sixty-five passengers and crew, had deviated from its normal flight pattern almost immediately after it had been instructed to another heading away from AA11. Instead of moving gradually north, parallel to the same track as AA11 was supposed to be traveling, it had been drifting south over the northwest shoulder of Connecticut when last seen on the air-traffic control scope. After it disappeared, the controller worriedly scanned the scope looking for the flight. "There's no transponder, no nothing, and no one's talking to him." [3]

Controllers began hearing disquieting transmissions from the first plane, AA11. Somehow someone said on the air-traffic control frequency: "We have some planes. Just stay quiet, and you'll be okay. We are returning to the airport." The confused controller replied, "Who's trying to call me?" Instead of a response, a voice from the plane apparently tried to quiet the passengers. "Nobody move please. We are going back to the airport. Don't try to make any stupid moves." [4]

No one knows for sure why these words were transmitted onto the air-traffic control communication frequency, but it gave the people listening on the ground the first tangible indication that something was very wrong on at least one of the flights. The person speaking could have thought the transmit button on the communication mike was connected to the public address system in the cabin, or there is speculation that before the pilot was completely overcome he had somehow, in a desperate silent call for help, keyed the mike open so the cockpit conversations would be audible to the controllers and caught on the tape system used for all air-traffic communications. After the first couple of transmissions, the controller at the Boston ARTCC put the transmissions on a speaker so others could hear them. He would say later that the voice chilled him and the words frightened him. The other plane, UA175, still on its drift south hadn't communicated with the controller in any manner.

It was approximately 8:41am. Alerted by the Boston ARTCC that at least one aircraft was not communicating and possibly had strayed out of the New England Region into Eastern Region airspace, controllers at the New York ARTCC began trying to track AA11 blindly because the plane's transponder was still deactivated.

Mike McCormick, the air-traffic manager at the New York ARTCC had been deep in thought working, while in the back of his mind savoring the past weekend. He had celebrated his birthday with his wife and eight-year-old son, Nicholas, by spending the entire weekend in Manhattan. On Saturday morning, the three of them had gotten up early and ventured to the World Trade Center so that his son could see the towers for the first time. They played silly games like putting their toes at the very base of the building and looking up at the impossibly tall towers, becoming dizzy in the process. They played in the fountain between the two giants while McCormick wondered about a friend's new job with the Port Authority. This new job would bring his friend to this very spot each day, beginning Monday.

The phone rang, pulling him out of his deep thoughts. It was the watch desk located on the floor of the control room, telling him of a possible hijack of a plane out of Boston. And, that it was probably heading south into their airspace.

In his twenty years with the agency, McCormick had never worked a real hijacking. Surely this would turn out like several others he had geared up for—a false alarm. He arrived at the watch desk location in time to be told, much to his surprise, it was "a confirmed hijacking with at least one dead and another injured." There were knives aboard.

The plane was heading south from Rochester, New York. A text page on his beeper had already told him that the plane was most likely AA11, which had last been seen at 31,000 feet and descending.

As controllers at the New York ARTCC peered at the screen trying to divine the position of the hidden airplane, one glanced up and yelled, "Look! There's an intruder over Allentown." [5] They had found the second plane while still not being able to locate the first. (Then the controller responsible for the air space where AA11 should have been switched to another radar system. The American aircraft jumped from the screen.) At 8:39am, it was at 29,000 feet, just passing over Albany.

Until now the controllers at the New York ARTCC had been confused as to the number of airplanes intruding into the New York airspace. Thinking that they were tracking the first and only missing plane, they were waiting for the inevitable hijacking scenario to unfold with demands. Then they realized, "I think we may be dealing with two aircraft here." [6]

McCormick was convinced that the communications systems on board AA11 had been damaged somehow—maybe a bomb had gone off leaving the plane's crew unable to talk to the controllers. He surmised that if the plane were in trouble, it might be making a run for a large airport with a long runway, such as Newark, New Jersey. He was convinced that the airplane's original crew was still in command and just trying to put the plane on the ground safely. He called the air-traffic manager at the New York TRACON, whose airspace would next be invaded.

Then as the ARTCC controllers and managers gathered around the scope and watched the actions of the plane—a small green blip on the radar screen—they all came to a chilling realization, "No, he's not going to land. He's going in." [7] Another said, "Oh, my God! He's headed for the city." And another, "Oh, my God! He's headed for Manhattan!" [8]

By now McCormick had begun adding up all the pieces and came up with what would be the correct answer—this was not an ordinary hijacking. He told the TRACON watch desk to look for other attacking planes. Transfixed with the scene unfolding on the bushel-basket-sized screen before them, the controllers at the New York ARTCC watched the inevitable happen. AA11's position was updated each time the radar sweep refreshed the screen until finally the plane disappeared. Someone reported that CNN was showing the hole that a small plane made as it hit the north tower of the World Trade Center. McCormick knew that it was actually a very large plane.

Hundreds of miles away, routine was quickly turning to trauma at the Boston ARTCC as they heard an uninvolved pilot high overhead key into a common frequency and ask: "Anybody know what that smoke is in Lower Manhattan?" [9] The pilot had just spotted the result of AA11 crashing into the north tower of the World Trade Center. Smoke and flames billowed out of all sides. The airplane had come in from the north, over the city, hitting the side of the building with such force that it had opened a huge wound all the way through the tower. Impossibly it sheared numerous sturdy steel beams—designed to stand guard thirty-nine inches apart all the way around the building's perimeter. A profile of the wing where the jet had entered the edifice was clearly apparent. Flames shot out in all directions. The world began to watch.

The controllers now saw that the second plane to be hijacked, UA175, was galloping southwest down the map, touching the southeast corner of New York until it entered northern New Jersey. Fixated on the intentions of the hijackers, McCormick knew that this plane too was going to crash. The waiting without being able to stop it was unbearable. In the minutes between the first crash and the second, he called the Eastern Region office informing them of the unfolding terror in the skies. He called the North American Aerospace Defense (NORAD) Command, asking them for assistance. He also shut down all plane departures from the entire region, making sure that no one could hijack another plane from his jurisdiction.

The New York ARTCC controllers watched as the anonymous blip that they knew was UA175 flew south. They realized that pilots Vic Saracini and Michael Horrocks were no longer at the helm because instead of showing the correct transponder code, the onboard system was transmitting a signature the computer didn't recognize. Unlike AA11, at least the controllers could see this plane without having to resort to the backup radar system. UA175 was far from its designated path and later it was learned flying at about five hundred miles an hour, roaring along the New York and New Jersey countryside. Just moments behind AA11, the second plane blazed a path, flying over the jewel-bright Hudson River. The river served as a great navigational aid, leading right to Manhattan. New York fire battalion commander Richard Picciotto later said, "I realize it was the beautiful day that killed us, because if it had been gray or foggy or overcast, there's no way those bastards could have flown those planes." [10]

As the controllers at the New York ARTCC tracked the blip, they realized, once again, that this wayward track was not the outcome of lost radio communications. Saying, "We may have a hijack. We have some problems over here right now," the controllers rapidly began to empty the airspace of all other planes, hoping to avoid a mid-air collision. [11] United Airlines 175 almost collided with another jet liner, a Delta Airlines flight, and moments later a US Airways airliner swerved out of its way after being notified by an onboard collision warning system of the approaching runaway. As UA175 touched New Jersey, the jumbo jet made a giant U-turn and moved toward the tip of Manhattan, flying from the southwest toward the northeast.

The United Airlines plane came over the water, low and fast. At 9:02am, as the first tower blazed, UA175 made a long, sweeping left curve, bucking up and down, but hanging to its inexorable grip on the target. It headed for the south tower of the World Trade Center. Just before it hit at over four hundred miles an hour, the pilot tilted the plane's wings slightly, ensuring they would slice through more floors and render the steel structure of the second building unstable. At air-traffic control in the New York ARTCC, the radar swept around, catching a shadow of the racing plane on each radar sweep. "Two, more hits…One more hit…That's the last. He's in." [12] Newark, New Jersey tower controller Rick Tepper had spotted the jet just before impact and while on the phone with another controller said, "Oh my God! He just hit the building," [13]

As the whole world watched on live television, glass blew out of the south tower. Airplane parts and engine pieces rained down on the streets. Paper, huge mountains of paper, floated in an impromptu confetti parade earthward, lingering on the breeze to dance in the crystal blue sky marred only by two cascades of fierce, black smoke. Tons of paper fell, leaving those still inside on the lower floors of the buildings wondering what was happening as the white sheets floated merrily by. When the north tower had been hit, alarms sounded in the south tower. After several moments, an all-clear announcement was given for people to return to their offices. Despite the noise of the hit on the first tower and the movement in the second tower due to the impact, none could see the damage and were still unknowing as to the emergency.

New York ARTCC manager McCormick realized that the danger might not be over yet. He and the air-traffic supervisors at the facility conferred. They had already halted all departures—that had happened seconds after AA11 had hit the north tower. Now that the second plane had crashed, he and the supervisors conferred again. Suggestions were made that ran the gamut of severity. It went from "Do we have the authority?" to "Land all of them!" After taking a few seconds to discuss it, they agreed. McCormick listened, then gave the order to land all arrivals within the airspace at the nearest feasible airports. He then instructed his operations managers that the entire airspace should go to "air traffic zero" thereby stopping all traffic from landing, taking off, or transiting through the New York airspace.

Shutting down all the airspace managed by an ARTCC was extremely rare and each incident costs the airlines millions of dollars. If McCormick guessed wrong as to the breadth of the attacks and had shut down his part of the system too rapidly, his and many of the air traffic managers' jobs would be on the line. Nearby, in other FAA facilities, air traffic controllers could see the burning towers. The smoke grew worse. A thousand things were going through their minds—mostly how to keep their wits about them so they could land the planes successfully. Get them down safely! Don't let the terrorists win another battle! One such location was the Newark, New Jersey air-traffic control tower. The height of the tower and its orientation gave those on duty a front-row seat to the devastation occurring in downtown Manhattan. They saw the first plane come from the north and moments later witnessed UA175 as it raced from the south and slammed into the second tower. Immediately, the air-traffic manager in the tower cancelled all traffic for that airport, departing and arriving. By now the controllers located in the Boston ARTCC had broken protocol and were warning every cockpit crew within their airspace to watch for danger.

New York ARTCC Deputy Air Traffic manager Bruce Barrett had worked with Mike McCormick frantically trying to make the right call for their airspace. He now worried about all of the planes heading toward New York City from overseas destinations. Rerouting them was going to be very difficult and he feared for them.

FAA investigation's manager Tony Ferrante landed safely in Chicago on Monday afternoon and was using his Tuesday morning commute time to the deposition hearing on current FAA litigation to check in with his wife in Virginia. His pager interrupted him with "Confirmed hijacking at Boston center." He told his wife about the page just as she was recounting to him the story of a small airplane that was being reported as having crashed into the north World Trade Center building. He turned into the parking lot of the Courtyard Hotel just as his pager went nuts with message after message telling him of the second hit. The big screen inside the hotel told him most of the rest of the story.

In an office in the FAA headquarters building in Washington, D.C., David Canoles, Director of Investigations and Evaluation, who had arrived at the FAA headquarters building on September 11 at his usual 5:30am, sat readying for the regular 7:15am meeting that was a rehash of operations issues from the day before. His daily efforts included litigation support for accidents from the government side and the management of a process quality-control group. While being involved in various court cases, personnel within his organization also spend months each year evaluating compliance of controllers to national standards of expertise. Various procedures, accident, and incident investigations need to be fully assessed, including near mid-air accidents if air-traffic personnel are involved. As a result, sixty evaluators spend twenty-six weeks a year on the road, watching controllers at work and checking training folders for training compliance.

Operational issues are a fact of life in air-traffic controlling. But there is a constant effort to upgrade the process, taking each opportunity for deviation away. As part of the procedure, all twenty-one of the ARTCCs are monitored through Canoles' organization. Every one of the centers' work force is responsible for the safe transit of a sizeable number of flights each day. For example, the Washington

ARTCC funnels the majority of commercial airline traffic either from or to every major airport on the east coast, managing around 8,000 flights a day. Any break from accepted procedures by a controller must be analyzed and corrected. These procedures have been developed through years of experience and testing and adherence to them is critical.

At around 8:15am Canoles received a text message on his beeper confirming a hijacking in progress. He knew this was not good, but he could do little except wait. Minutes after contemplating the message scrawled across his liquid crystal screen, he frowned as he looked up from his desk. On the muted television screen in his office, tuned to CNN, he saw a replay of the results of the first World Trade Center crash. The camera panned to the top of the tower, showing the smoke as it poured from the wound. Canoles saw the outline of the damage and knew, despite what the now louder volume was saying about the size of the intruder, the iconic building had been hit by a very large airplane. He ran toward the Deputy Administrator's office on the tenth floor, meeting acting air-traffic manager, Jeff Griffith on the way. Griffith rerouted him saying, "Go and start a command center," putting into motion a telephone conference that was to last for over a year. It became the never-ending teleconference (telcon).

Canoles had just left a regular staff meeting with some of the personnel who worked for him on the fourth floor of the FAA's headquarters building. They discussed the operational hot items that had occurred in the system within the last twenty-four hours as well as the litigation issues each was pursuing. Tony Mello, Assistant Investigations Manager, was still in the desk bay area. Canoles zipped by, with these terse words: "Let's go. We've had a hijacking."

Mello was startled. He, like most of the others in the organization who had arrived at around 5:30am, was expecting a normal day of tracking operational issues throughout the system, He had done his homework earlier that morning working through reports of all the operations anomalies from the previous twenty-four hours and had helped put together the report always presented at the 7:15am air-traffic meeting.

Canoles and Mello hurried to the Air Traffic manager's suite of rooms on the tenth floor of the FAA's headquarters building. In the conference room they opened up the phone lines on the black disk-type phone located on the table and set up a command post. They immediately called the FAA Command Center in Northern Virginia, and the New England, Eastern, and Great Lakes regional offices. Mike McCormick, New York ARTCC manager was one of the first on the telcon, briefing those listening about the situation in the New York City area. McCormick had already secured the ARTCC facility by locking all the doors and requesting police protection. He had arranged for counselors and ministers to be available to everyone, especially the controllers who had been involved in tracking the crashed planes. His highest priority then focused on the five managers from his facility who were on various forms of travel. He instructed that all of them be found and requested to return to the building. His main and most intense worry: the two who were on familiarization travel, which meant that they were riding in the cockpits of commercial jets.

The telcon was originally intended to reach only this small audience, but soon mushroomed into a national forum. Questions multiplied. The situation began to involve the entire country. Each ARTCC was rapidly routed into the call, with the larger regional facilities, the TRACONs, joining later. The top tier of the FAA headquarters management structure surrounded the wooden table, anxiously listening to the field managers. Questions peppered the telephone line as everyone tried to conjure a tactical sense of the state of the system.

Canoles paced the room, trying to get an overview. Each manager was asked to give the status of every airplane within their airspace, indicating if anything was amiss in anyone's response to air-traffic control instructions. Soon the group was joined by the onsite Department of Defense (DoD) liaison to the FAA. As the picture began resolving itself, Mello wondered if the very building within which they sat might be the next target. Canoles reminded everyone that whatever was said, any instructions given, must be remembered and recorded. A white marking board already in the conference room was used at first as the notepad. Later an exact listing of all questions and answers were meticulously committed to a laptop computer.

Air Traffic Planning and Procedures manager, Mike Cirillo had just completed his first meeting of the morning when he was tersely instructed to report to the Air Traffic suite of offices as well. He had just heard an incredible rumor that a plane had hit one of the World Trade Center towers. As he hurried toward the tenth floor, he quickly changed focus from his daily tasks to an emergency action mode.

Cirillo had spent the last few weeks engrossed in the implications of a new strategic document produced by the FAA. His management responsibilities cover air-traffic procedures and the Operations Evolution Plan (OEP) contained sweeping changes. Two of the measures with which he was wrestling were the closely spaced parallel runways process and the land and hold short at intersecting runways procedure. Both were outside the cultural norm for the aviation industry and Cirillo was trying to determine if they could be executed. Suddenly jerked back from the future, he dropped everything and raced up the four floors to the executive suite.

Bill Peacock had returned to his hotel room. He flipped through the channels and found CNN just in time to join the world in viewing the attack on the second tower. He determinedly dialed the phone, trying to connect with his staff. His call was routed to the phone in the conference room next door to his office at headquarters, into the never-ending teleconference. His deputy Jeff Griffith was serving as liaison to FAA Deputy Monte Belger, trying to gather a tactical notion of the attacks. Peacock's first questions to the air traffic managers at every major controlling facility in the U.S. determined what security measures had been executed. He quickly gathered the few of his staffers traveling with him in New Orleans as things went into rapid-fire mode. They knew two planes had already crashed and were quickly informed of another possible hijacking. This would turn out to be UA93.

Frank Hatfield, who had admired the beautiful sky moments earlier in the day, left his office building near JFK Airport on Long Island. He too had been advised earlier that morning by the New York ARTCC that a possible hijacking was in progress, but years had passed since an alarm had resulted in a real takeover. Besides no one on the plane had squawked the hijack code (turned the transponder to read 7500). It was a small red flag in his day, but a false sense of security had enveloped him as it had the entire nation. At about 8:45am, within moments of the first crash into the World Trade Center, Hatfield's beeper alerted him of the attack. By the time he made a U-turn and was able to return to the regional office, his staff had already begun forming a crisis center, setting up a telcon with all the major air-traffic control facilities within his management reach—New York and Washington ARTCCs, JFK, LaGuardia, Newark, Reagan National, Philadelphia, Baltimore-Washington International, and Dulles air-traffic control towers, plus several regional-level controlling facilities.

Even as Hatfield raced back toward his FAA office, he knew in his heart of hearts that this was no accident. There were no clouds. Experienced controllers were on the boards. "Maybe," he thought, "it was a general aviation airplane with someone at the controls who had suffered a heart attack!" He discounted that almost immediately. Before news of the second airplane crash reached him, he had already decided the U.S. and more importantly, New York City, was under a terrorist attack. He prayed for the collision to be mechanical failure or medical mishap. As news of the second crash reached him, he knew his first impulse had been correct.

Inside the regional office, the quiet was deafening. People hunkered down in groups, quietly trying to understand the extent of the attack. The regional facility telcon was under way and everyone had begun searching for other "lost" airplanes. The number of potential planes that had been hijacked was fluid in those first few minutes. If even a suspicion existed of the plane being under foreign influence, it was reported.

Then the Eastern Region managers tied into the never-ending telcon being conducted from the Air Traffic conference room, reporting what they knew to headquarters.

Washington ARTCC air traffic manager Luis Ramirez had gotten to work on Tuesday at his normal 6:30am. Being forever attracted to his initial calling of controlling air traffic, he walked the control room floor as he did every day at about 7:00am just to feel the atmosphere of the action. He greeted controllers, checking the numbers present on September 11, making sure every seat was occupied and that his facility had a full contingent of one hundred professionals.

This facility was one of the first few of its type to be opened by the federal government. Seventh in the line of control centers, the operation was originally commissioned on April 1, 1937 and has been in service ever since. The building had changed, but people had been controlling traffic from Washington ARTCC for seventy-four years.

After twenty-one years with the FAA, Ramirez focused during the last ten months on lowering the operational errors at this major facility. As he worked with the controller management and union representative each week, they tried to determine any cause for controllers' errors and manage them with training. The error rate had begun to dissipate and he was pleased. Like him, the controllers on duty loved the order of the process. Each day, those at the Washington ARTCC and thousands of others just like them deftly moved five hundred thousand pound Kitty Hawk progeny across the sky in such a manner that the controllers were basically background music. Only if a controller makes a wrong move do the passengers ever realize that someone other than the pilot is helping to guide their plane.

Ramirez walked into the cavernous control room, its darkness contrasted by the soft glow of the controllers' scopes. A distinctive smell always accompanied the large banks of electronics—part warm rubber and part metal. The gloom makes the high ceiling unnoticeable. The murmuring of each controller as they quietly give orders to the pilots of airplanes high overhead adds to the cocoon affect. As the controllers manage the skies, they roll from side to side in wheeled office chairs handling the scope showing the radar sweep and the paper work of each airplane as it enters and leaves the sector of airspace they control. In this facility, one hundred controllers per watch manipulate the airplanes while supervisors look on. Weather and delay information from all over the nation is fed to every position ensuring that each controller has a 360-degree web of awareness. Their headsets on, they key the mike of the communications equipment and dance with the sky.

The modern controller's suite of equipment is anchored by a computer display on a softly backlit screen showing the positions of every aircraft under his or her direction. Fed by a complex computer system that helps them keep tabs on each airplane in their designated airspace. Sophisticated surveillance equipment feeds this screen from radars located throughout the region and ultimately the nation. Communication is facilitated through modern equipment—not like in the old days.

In 1938, as the centers were being established, en route air traffic control was a very new science and little controlling was done, mostly data exchange, giving each pilot an idea as to the traffic as he approached a particular area. Party-line telephones were used to contact local airline radio ground stations and control towers, with radio range stations relaying the location information to the proper individuals. On June 30, 1938, the Department of Commerce initiated a teletype network so that centers, airway communications stations, and military bases  could communicate on a dedicated system. While the communications equipment was simple at best, the controlling hardware was even less sophisticated. Early control methodology consisted of a person standing near the runway with colored flags waving green to signal the pilot to proceed in taking off or landing and red to hold. [14]

Navigation was just as rudimentary. Commencing in the early 1920s, as the fledgling aviation industry found its way through various national fads, its most useful mission was moving mail rapidly across the country. Initially, planes could only fly during the daytime, in good weather, which didn't speed the mail across the country any more rapidly than trains could. Actually in some cases, airmail was slower than train mail. Radar hadn't been invented and sophisticated navigation equipment was years away. As experiments were run on moving mail at night along designated routes, solutions as simple as large wood-burning bonfires provided navigation aids for the pilots. Finally, rotating light beacons were placed on some of the routes to guide the pilots on short hops about the country.

On the morning of September 11, in the Washington ARTCC, moments after completing his stroll through the control room floor and returning to his office, Ramirez received a phone call from Mike McCormick at the New York ARTCC telling him about one of the suspected hijackings. Since the plane had been headed for airspace controlled by Washington ARTCC, the New York manager had called as a courtesy, not wanting the rogue airplane to possibly take the Washington controllers by surprise. His normally happy features clouded, Ramirez wheeled and returned to the control room. There, he was informed that a plane had hit the north tower of the World Trade Center. He sprinted down the hall from the control room to the supervisor's break room and flipped the television to CNN.

He saw the smoke and destruction. He headed for his office, but hadn't made it that far when his secretary told him that a second airplane had hit the World Trade Center, this time the south tower. For the third time, he ran back to the control room, arriving just in time to hear the New York ARTCC declare, "ATC zero," meaning that the entire airspace managed by that facility would accept no more airplanes into its airspace. Mike McCormick, at the New York ARTCC, had declared the center's airspace closed. Moments later Ramirez heard that the entire Eastern Region airspace was closed to all inbound airplanes—a huge block of countryside and airspace ranging from New York to West Virginia and Virginia, affecting his center.

Washington Reagan National Airport is part of that airspace and it was where FAA employee Larry Bicknell had boarded the Tuesday 7:30am shuttle to LaGuardia. The air traffic manager at Reagan National, Bicknell was headed to the Eastern Regional office, located in the New York City area where he was scheduled to attend a management meeting. Shortly before 9:00am Bicknell left the LaGuardia terminal, hailed a cab, and headed south to the meeting, traveling away from the World Trade Center skyscraper that was in flames, oblivious to its dire straits.

That day, Bicknell, who has since retired from federal service, was the manager of all the controllers at Reagan National Airport where about 1,000 operations occur each day. (Dulles has 1,600 operations and BWI has 950) Just as he arrived at the FAA's local office, he saw a television screen show the second airplane slam into the south tower. Stopped in his tracks, he immediately understood the implications. He hurried to the air traffic manager's office to determine where he could lend a hand. Thirty years of controlling traffic and managing operations had supplied him with intuition enough to know that the entire air-traffic control system was in danger. He dialed into the never-ending telcon. Bicknell and Ed McKenna from Syracuse spent long hours manning the phone speaker, helping answer questions and relay messages to regional personnel. Late in the evening, he and several others were sent to a local hotel to get some sleep, knowing that some of them would have to return to help man the mid-watch. As a precaution on the night of September 11, in addition to the New York ARTCC, the Boston ARTCC, the nineteen additional centers located throughout the nation began sitting watches on the telcon, making each facility instantaneously available for crisis management if new events unfolded.

At the Eastern Region office, Frank Hatfield began giving orders. First, he needed someone to keep a record of decisions in writing—a list of what question was asked by whom and who responded with what answer. So many instructions, queries, and commands were being given that only a written record would ensure that no mistakes were made. This office was the major FAA facility nearest the first attacks and they were in the maelstrom of information gathering. The demands grew. As Hatfield realized where the attacks were taking place, his worries grew for all the controllers manning locations within view of the distressed buildings. He said later, that even though most of the controllers at the three major New York City airports could see the smoke and flames pouring from the two buildings and later saw the collapse, not a single one abandoned his stations. Many had friends or family within the towers, but remained loyal to the airplanes, containing thousands of passengers, still trying to land. His worries multiplied when he realized how intensely personal the attacks were to everyone in the FAA. Controllers, supervisors, analysts, and hundreds of others began to feel the anger that visited them repeatedly in the days to come—that someone could use their system as a weapon was unfathomable. He said later that he was "so proud to have worked with all the FAA people that day." The atmosphere in all the operational spaces throughout his management sphere, despite all the worries, was intensely professional and became more determined at each turn.

Rick Hostetler, a member of the FAA's Planning and Procedures organization, was sitting in the dentist's chair having a root canal performed as the television showed the first World Trade Center tower in flames. His first thought was, "My God. What a horrible accident!" As he saw the second one hit, his military background gave him the instincts to immediately surmise that the U.S. was under attack from a foreign power. The dentist, a former military officer, was also looking at the damage being shown by CNN, and without a word began doing a patch job on the root canal.

Hostetler's job includes acting as the FAA's primary air-traffic liaison for the Secret Service, the United States Special Operations Command, and the Pentagon. He makes sure that the FAA is properly represented and that air-traffic rules and temporary flight restrictions are communicated to everyone who needs them during national security events such as the Super Bowl and United Nations' meetings. He left Waldorf, Maryland and drove into the teeth of the traffic as everyone fled downtown Washington, D.C. and tried to navigate into Northern Virginia to his duty station at the Command Center. His beeper and secure cell phone were screaming for attention as he drove.

Before and during the attacks on New York City, passenger jets had continued in the normal pattern, taking off from hundreds of airports all over the U.S. One of them at an airport near Washington, loading at the mid-terminal gate D26 was a Boeing 757 serving as American Airlines Flight 77 (AA77) carrying sixty-four people. It lifted off from Dulles International Airport en route to Los Angeles at 8:20am, several minutes before the first plane crashed into the World Trade Center Towers. Captain Charles Burlingame climbed the jet toward its cruising altitude of 35,000 feet while being handed off through a series of controllers, from the Dulles tower, to the Dulles TRACON, then the Washington ARTCC, and as he traveled across the country, the Indianapolis ARTCC. The Indianapolis controller had given Burlingame directions for the giant Boeing plane to fly via the VOR located near Falmouth, Kentucky. Pilot confirmation of the controller's instructions had been routine. Then communication ceased. At 8:56am, an Indianapolis ARTCC controller called repeatedly to the silent airplane, "American 77, Indy." Then, the pattern began repeating itself as the plane's transponder went silent, no longer transmitting its identification information on the controllers' screens.

Something was amiss. The plane went AWOL in an area of coverage supported by radar that only reports based on information broadcast from a transponder. So when the transponder blacked out, no other way of seeing the plane existed.

Much of the airspace in the United States is covered by two kinds of radar—the type that lists transponder information (secondary) and the kind that "sees" the airplane by shooting a beam at it. This type reads the bounce back (primary), and gives information to the controller confirming the location of an airplane. So when the transponder was turned off on American 77 by the hijackers and the flight information ceased to show on the screen, there was no other manner available by which to track the rogue plane. The FAA called American Airline's company dispatch office in Dallas asking them to raise them on the company communication equipment. "We called [the] company. They can't even get ahold of him," complained a controller. [15] Unaware of the terror going on in New York City, by 9:09am, the controller thought either the airplane had experienced a massive electrical failure and was flying along its original path, unable to be heard, or it had crashed. Assuming the plane could still be flying blindly along its original path, the controller cleared all other aircraft from the plane's heading.

In what was to be one of the few major communication errors of the day, when the Indianapolis ARTCC supervisor called the regional operations center to report the loss of communication with AA77, a flight service station employee picked up on the communication and called the Ashland, Kentucky, police to report a confirmed crash. The ARTCC controllers had noted the last known position of AA77, near the Ohio/Kentucky border. This became part of the report. As other FAA personnel were trying to determine whether any unidentified crashes had been reported to local police, Indianapolis ARTCC personnel contacted the same police office asking for information on any crashes. The local police, using the flight service station report as an actual accident, confirmed a crash that never happened, creating mass confusion. A state helicopter was dispatched to the plane's last coordinates, only there wasn't any downed airplane. Instead of crashing, the plane was hijacked, the transponder turned off, and the plane had doubled back toward Washington. Time had been lost in all the confusion and the plane had completely disappeared in the area with only secondary radar coverage.

Even pilots on planes that were not hijacked became uneasy. Pilot Dave Lubore began September 11 in Miami. With him sitting in the right seat, his Airbus A-320 had taken off on its way to Pittsburgh long before the hijackings had occurred. They were cruising over western North Carolina when air-traffic controllers calling from the Washington ARTCC reported a problem at the New York ARTCC—about the time of the first World Trade Center crash. Lubore then heard the same controllers divert a Delta Airlines jet from its path into New York airspace, asking it to return to its airport of origin—Atlanta. Something significant was amiss. The radio came alive again. Another aircraft was diverted after being told that all of the New York airspace was closed. Soon after, Lubore's Airbus received a short, but terse instruction from someone on the frequency, presumably an air-traffic controller telling all of them to "...lock your doors."

The startled crew continued to push the Airbus north toward Pittsburgh. Soon after, as the airplane was closing in on the North Carolina/Virginia border, they were told that the Pittsburgh air-traffic control tower had been evacuated and was not accepting any traffic. The flight crew looked at each other. What was going on? Was the U.S. being attacked by another country—possibly with nuclear weapons? Now they had no destination. The two pilots conferred with their company's operations control through ACARS, a computer data-link system, and decided on Cleveland as their alternate destination. The Washington ARTCC controllers denied their request for clearance for Cleveland (it was also closed), telling them to land as soon as they could, suggesting Roanoke, Virginia. Lubore knew that while the A-320 would fit on the runway adequately, the Roanoke airport had several obstacles near the approach path that must be avoided in order to successfully land. Because neither he nor the pilot flew there regularly, they didn't carry the navigation plates that showed the obstacles.

As they approached Roanoke, Lubore contacted Washington ARTCC controllers again, requesting Dulles, Virginia, as their destination. The ACARS was humming as the pilots fed each new destination into the communication equipment, alerting the home office of the potential changes in their landing instructions. Everyone agreed on Dulles. They flew north toward northern Virginia. The air-traffic controller gave them clearance to descend as they were about forty miles from the end of the runway, only to have to tell them minutes later that the airport had just been closed. By now the pilots had changed courses for three different airports—Cleveland, Roanoke, and Dulles—but still hadn't been told what was happening. They climbed back to cruising altitude, gently nudging the airplane in a giant, clockwise circle. They heard a pilot in a jet behind them in the approach queue call Dulles with a "min fuel" declaration, indicating that his airplane didn't have enough fuel to accept the diversion. Dulles air-traffic control relented, letting him line up for final approach and land. Lubore's plane was still looking for a destination.

Lubore searched his memory for nearby airports that could handle the landing and fueling requirements of his airplane and suggested Richmond, Virginia. The company and air-traffic control both agreed. Company operations had told them through ACARS that a "major problem" was happening, but didn't elaborate. Finally, as they straightened out of their long circle and contacted the Richmond TRACON, the controller guiding them toward the runway told them what was happening. She recounted the litany of horrors that had occurred in the nearly three hours they had been aloft—that both towers at the World Trade Center had been hit and had fallen. Both the pilot and copilot were horrified. Had up to

50,000 people had been lost? As the controller continued with the details, the pilot asked Lubore to stop her, worrying that he might not be able to concentrate and land the plane safely if he knew too many of the details.

The giant A-320 glided toward the tarmac, landing safely. Only after the plane was taxiing toward the mostly empty terminal did the cockpit crew tell the passengers that they had landed in Richmond, Virginia. So smoothly had they handled the twisting and turning of each destination change, no one was aware that he hadn't just landed at the Pittsburgh airport. Then the pilot told them the rest of what he knew.

Edgy controllers throughout the nation began reporting all failed transponders as possible hijackings. Transponders fail during flight sometimes, but as this day progressed any "normal" occurrence of this was immediately suspect. Each suspected hijacking was monitored by the facility in control of its immediate airspace. As it turned out, none of the other transponder failures noted later in the day was the result of additional hijackings.

Refusing to become spectators, FAA air-traffic director Peacock and his staff anxiously began trying to determine the health of the air-traffic system. He concentrated on keeping the thirteen thousand controllers in position to control the other five thousand airplanes still in the air, while watching for any trends portending another onslaught by terrorists. Everyone was expecting a second wave and wanted to be able to spot it before it became uncontrollable. So, they continued to watch.

4

Sabra Kaulia, manager of the FAA's Air Traffic Airspace Management (ATA-1), walked into the regular 9:00am Tuesday morning just in time to see the television show the second airplane crash into the south tower of the WTC. All the meeting regulars were there and by now very upset, having already seen the damaged north tower engulfed in flames and smoke. Kaulia heard someone say that a Cessna had torn through the first tower. But how could a small plane have lost its way and run into such a large building on such a clear day? CNN cameras zoomed in, showing the extent of the tears in the skin of the north tower and she immediately realized that this much damage couldn't have been caused by a small, general aviation airplane. Then someone in the room hazarded a guess that it had been a Boeing 737, at least.

Moments ago, her most pressing work issue had been how to support the airspace redesign effort in order to create more capacity in the National Airspace System. The people in her organization had been planning all the airspace and procedure modifications they would be doing during the next year. Just recently promoted to the position, Kaulia was having a great time learning all it entailed. Capacity issues were plaguing the FAA and part of her job was to help find ways to allow more airplanes to enter the nation's airspace during the next year.

Someone suggested that the first airplane had experienced an emergency or a mechanical problem, causing it to crash. But because the second airplane had hit the other building she knew that both were intentional. A thought, unbidden sprang to her mind: "Someone brought it home to us!" She didn't know whom the "someone" was, but was horrified at how many people, from the planes alone, might be dead and began grieving for each of them. As the smoke and flames poured across the television screen, she began rooting for the rescue operations, thinking they had minutes, even hours to get everyone out of the towers. She hurried to the Air Traffic office suite on the tenth floor and knew this was the beginning of a fierce fight against an enemy no one knew and became part of the never-ending telephone conference.

As the first two hijackings played out, the FAA contacted the Pentagon, coordinating information on the attacks, determining what the military response was going to be. At 8:38am, a few minutes before the first tower was hit, the North

American Aerospace Defense Command had been called. For years during the Cold War, planes and pilots had stood constantly at the ready to ward off any airborne intruders. In the years since the declaration of peace between the super power nations, only about twenty planes stand ready on a daily basis, at seven air bases nationwide. Some of these were now being called to service.

Two fighter jets with pilots stood on alert at Otis Air Base at Cape Cod, Massachusetts. At 8:43am the FAA notified the 102nd Fighter Wing of the Massachusetts Air National Guard that AA11 had probably been hijacked. The F-15 airplanes were scrambled just as the jumbo jet was burying itself in the north tower of the WTC. The sleek fighter jets jumped off the runway, almost straight up, heading for New York at top speed—it would take only fifteen minutes. Tension filled the pilots' world. They had finally been scrambled, but the enemy was already past the gate. Word of the hijacking of UA175 was passed up to them. They fire-walled the throttles on their planes all the way there, but were seventy miles away when the second aircraft hit. Speeding at twelve miles per minute, they came into view of New York City too late to stop the plane from plunging into the second tower, getting a front row seat of both towers in flames. Not sure if other planes were heading toward the beleaguered city, they flew on station for hours, circling the black smoke and rubble below, warding off any intruders into the air space. [1]

Back at Dulles, controllers spotted an anomaly on their scopes. An unidentified plane, its transponder mute, streaked west to east in their airspace—airspace that had primary radar coverage. Convinced that it had crashed somewhere in Kentucky, controllers had jettisoned American Airlines 77 from their minds, worrying about all the airplanes still in the air. By now Middle Eastern men on flight AA77 had announced to the passengers that they were hijacking the plane. The pilot, reportedly after desperate hand-to-hand combat, was killed, leaving his plane of people unprotected and in the hands of terrorists. The passengers were dealing with the reality that they had been hijacked long before the controllers saw the airplane as it jetted back toward the capital. Not until the plane reentered airspace controlled by the Dulles TRACON, did anyone realize it was still in the air, hurtling toward downtown Washington. At 9:25am a controller at Dulles saw the unidentified plane as a green icon shooting across her scope. Its trajectory would take it directly to the White House.

The FAA called the White House immediately warning them of the incoming airplane. The president was out of town, but Vice President Dick Cheney was sitting in his office when at 9:32am Secret Service agents burst in saying, "Sir, we have to leave immediately." [2] They grabbed him under both arms and raced him from the room, down to the underground bunker, convinced that the White House was the next target. Soon Norman Mineta, the Transportation Secretary, joined him. Mineta tapped into a communication line at the FAA Operations Center where AA77's flight path was being monitored—waiting seven long seconds for each new radar sweep to show them where the airplane was headed.

According to a few cell phone calls coming from passengers on AA77, all of them had been herded to the back of the airplane. Some learned the fate of the other two airplanes in New York City. Everyone on the ground had already heard or seen the second plane crash into the south tower in New York and some thought it might have been AA77. It had been UA175 instead.

Now the Dulles flight's track was taking it directly toward the White House and the no-fly zone surrounding most of the federal buildings in downtown. Washington Dulles controllers called Reagan National Airport notifying them of the incoming plane; it would be in National's air space soon, causing trouble for that airport's inbound and outbound traffic within minutes. The alarm was given. The Air Traffic headquarters telcon was informed of the inbound plane. As the location was described, Dave Canoles realized it was virtually on top of their downtown location where the never-ending telcon was taking place. Mike McCormick, located in the New York ARTCC, but listening to everything via the telcon said, "Are you going to be okay where you are?" He would say later that he thought everyone in that room was very brave to have continued, knowing that the plane might be heading straight for their building. Canoles dispatched Jeff Loague to look for the jet out the window of the next-door office.

He said, "See if you can spot it." Canoles himself was concerned that the plane might be headed for the boxy building housing the FAA, but refused to yield to the hijackers. Procedures manager Cirillo was also in the office speaking directly to federal law enforcement, relaying to them the location of the plane. Someone tied into the telcon from Dulles was giving a slow count of the plane's distance from the White House in miles, "forty, thirty, twenty." It went fast, but slow. The plane moved rapidly, but seemed to take forever to reach them.

Finally, Loague yelled, "I see something!" As the plane was spotted north of the building, executing a long, sort of lazy turn, circling its prey, everyone held his breath. Cirillo tensely continued translating the countdown to federal personnel down the street. Then Loague picked up the commentary, anxiously describing the scene as the plane lost altitude until the glint of the silver fuselage was lost in the ground clutter of the residences and office buildings surrounding the Pentagon. He breathed, "Oh, my God!" as the smoke rushed up from the ground into his line of vision.

A C-130, recently airborne from Andrews Air Force Base, had been requested to look out for AA77 and spotted the big jet, confirming that it was flying low and fast. The shiny plane was actually moving at around five hundred miles an hour. The C-130 pilots reported the same scene that the FAA observer was seeing. It streaked across the sky. Going over the White House, and nearing the Capitol, the giant behemoth seemed to realize it had overrun its target. Correcting itself, the plane started a long ominous, clockwise spiral. Losing altitude, circling until it was southwest of the Pentagon, it hugged the terrain, like a giant raptor stalking its quarry. In the last few seconds it crested the hill just west of the Pentagon, skimmed over Arlington Village and the Navy Annex almost within touching range of the orderly rows of white headstones in Arlington National Cemetery. It flew straight over the Pentagon helicopter pad, trimming off tops of trees and light poles, smashing an engine generator building, barely above the ground, landing wheels up, crashing into the west wall of the Pentagon. People inside heard a split second of the frenzied whine of the jets and saw the shadow darken some of the windows just before impact.

Nearly 45,000 pounds of jet fuel burst into an aerosol, immediately becoming a huge mass of orange and blue flames. This pushed a wave of air, smoke, and heat through the halls and offices, creating another parade of paper fluttering aimlessly in front of a wave of air pressure. People felt the heat and smelled the aviation fuel. A wall of smoke billowed up from the seriously injured building. Windows were blown out all along the 921-foot granite wall of the west side. Huge parts of concrete were blown away or crumbled into dust as the plane burrowed into the structure. Hundreds of the 41,492 columns that make up the giant building's foundation were damaged and a section of it began collapsing. A giant fireball rose into the sky, black smoke following. The heat was intense both inside and out. Trees burned—aluminum shards falling from the sky smoked with heat. The time was 9:38am, thirty-six minutes after the last crash in New York City.

In the White House bunker, an explosion reported from the Pentagon confirmed for the government's executives the final target of the jet. F-16s from Langley Air Force Base in Hampton, Virginia had scrambled at 9:30am in response to the danger, hurrying first toward New York City then back toward Washington. Like the fighter planes in New York City, they arrived too late. Their job, after learning AA77 had crashed, was confirming for their commanders that the Pentagon was aflame. Then they were told to fly on station over the White House, guarding it against all comers at all cost, until given further orders.

Moments later, Transportation Secretary Mineta yelled at Monte Belger, acting Deputy Administrator of the FAA, also on the communications line: "Monte, bring all the planes down." Reassuring the Secretary that the action was already in process on many fronts, Belger said, "We're bringing them down per pilot discretion." (Airline pilots always have the responsibility for the safety of their craft and can make decisions counter to air-traffic control instructions when they deem it necessary.) Not today. Mineta said, "[Expletive] pilot discretion. Get those goddamn planes down." [3]

Unknown to Secretary Mineta and the rest of the country, even before the Pentagon attack a series of actions shutting the system down had already been executed by FAA managers throughout the stricken East Coast. Washington's Reagan National Airport managers, upon hearing of the New York City crashes, risking later rebuke, had banned all VFR (general aviation) flights from the airspace within their jurisdiction, clearing controller scopes of all extraneous data except for commercial airliners. After the third crash, all staff from the air-traffic control tower at Reagan were evacuated except for a couple of supervisors who stayed to ensure that emergency issues and communications were managed. The country was under attack, jet planes used as missiles, and there seemed to be nothing that anyone could do to stop it.

Because of the intuition of dozens of managers, supervisors, and controllers, long before Secretary Mineta gave the command, the "land all planes" order already permeated the system. Despite its uniqueness, several of the major controlling organizations had already begun executing actions that would protect their local settlements, both large and small. Airline executives reacted, landing their companies' airplanes before more damage could be done. American Airline's Craig Marquis gave the order for his airline, barking, "Anything that hasn't taken off in the Northeast, don't take off." [4]

Someone at the Boston ARTCC gave the order to ground all the airplanes at the airports within the center's jurisdiction just minutes after the second New York crash. It was an unusual step, affecting so many planes, but it immediately took several hundred airplanes out of the hijacking equation. No other potential victims were allowed to leave the ground and the air space was cleared ensuring that as a by-product of the tensions of the day, no compounding accidents would occur.

Eastern Region managers saw the pattern of danger quickly evolving and by 9:09am the New York ARTCC manager Mike McCormick had grounded the planes within his jurisdiction. The regional air-traffic manager Frank Hatfield ordered a regional ground stop. Headquarters agreed. So all the airplanes in the air in the entire region—New York, Pennsylvania, New Jersey, Delaware, Maryland, Virginia, and West Virginia—were grounded. Those on the ground were forced to stay there. None flying from other regions toward these states were allowed to enter the airspace. All planes in the air within this area were told to leave or land, thereby "sterilizing" the airspace of all but warplanes. Great Lakes and New England followed in short order, starting a domino affect of shutting down airspace nationwide.

At the Washington ARTCC, Air Traffic manager Ramirez was also already in action. In rapid-fire mode, he had ordered a ground stop of all airplanes within his control—meaning those at all the airports from which the center's controllers would be accepting airplanes. Someone in the control room challenged his authority to take this kind of action, but he did it anyway. If necessary, he'd ask for forgiveness later. He called the FAA's national command center, coordinating the action with them. Approximately ten minutes later, at 9:29am, a notice to airmen (NOTAM) announced a national ground stop that prevented the takeoff of all civil aircraft, no matter where they were or where they were going. Ramirez and the controller's local union leader spoke to each controller, instructing them to tell each of the approximately 1,000 planes showing on the center's scopes to "…pick an airport and land." Reinforcing that command, they told the controllers if anyone questioned the order, tell them it's a matter of "national security."

Ramirez's deputy, Ken Myers, was at Dulles airport on board an airplane—destination New York City. Luis paged him. "Airplane hit twin towers in New York City. RTB [return to base] immediately." At the moment of the cancellation of the flights, Myers' plane had already pulled away from the gate, delaying him from disembarking for several hours until a gate became available.

Despite some reticence by pilots and airline companies, within an hour all the planes in the airspace controlled by the Washington ARTCC were on the ground. That completed, the managers began thinking about the mental state of their personnel.

Deputy Air Traffic manager Myers finally arrived, joining Ramirez and the center's union representative. They began developing a plan to relieve all the controllers so they could go to their families. Like many of the other major air-traffic control facilities in the country that morning, the Washington ARTCC had been locked down and sharp shooters were on the roof soon after the attacks began. Tension was high and for a while no one was allowed in or out. Ramirez remembers that after the professional persona of the controllers was allowed to slip, after all the planes had been safely landed, he saw shock and fright on the controllers' faces. The expression was mirrored in everyone's heart. Luis also began gathering information as to which of his personnel might have been most affected by the assault—those who had family members on airplanes, or who lived near towns that according to rumor might still be under attack. They were frightened for their families, their system, and their country, so he began to gate them out of the facility as he could spare them. As the morning wore on, he gave himself a few minutes to make a single call reassuring himself that his wife, who works in downtown Washington, was safely away from what still might become the third ground zero.

Just as in Washington, controllers working at all of the twenty-one ARTCCs in the United States were busily pulling planes from the air. Instinctively, many of them had begun doing so as soon as the real action in New York City became clear. Twenty-plus year FAA air-traffic controller Kevin Kiss, an en route controller at the Ft. Worth ARTCC, had just returned from break and began moving the planes in his care around and through the West Texas sectors and the southwest corner post into Dallas-Ft. Worth Airport. Another controller walked through the floor, telling everyone that a small plane had hit the World Trade Center in New York City. Kiss, the son of a former air-traffic controller and air-traffic manager, decided that such an incident was probably a general aviation plane that had wandered off track in low visibility and thought the outcome was probably going to be more spectacular than serious. His rush hour in the sky hadn't hit yet, so he controlled mostly metro props and general aviation, including a couple of VFR flights that were going to Austin and San Antonio. The controllers on the scopes were notified that the second tower had been hit.

Supervisors began to hurry throughout the floor telling all the controllers to "get everyone out of the sky now!" "Tell them to land at the nearest airport."

Kiss advised all of his planes to determine the nearest airport and land. Many, both general aviation and commercial jets, didn't know how to take the order. Some began landing procedures immediately. So unprecedented was the command that others had to be convinced of the need to land. Finally, one general aviation plane declined completely, saying he wanted to continue to San Antonio—nearly two hours away from his current location. Kiss insisted that the plane land. The pilot requested a change from IFR status to VFR, thinking that if he was no longer under controller watch that his problems would be solved. As the small plane's pilot continued to wheedle his way through the air, Kiss contacted a supervisor for instructions and then told the pilot that if he didn't land at the nearest airport, the military was willing to scramble and if necessary shoot down his plane. The frequency became very quiet. The pilot conceded that landing at Waco would probably be a good idea and proceeded to clear the sky.

National Air Traffic Control Association president John Carr noted that this was a problem nation wide. He said, "There were more than a few instances where controllers had to talk pilots into understanding what they were being directed to do." [5] Others understood, but were all too aware of the consequences to the company if a big jet was landed at somewhere other than a hub normally used by the company. The plane would be out of sequence when needed somewhere else, causing a ripple through the entire system when they were allowed to fly again, so many of them pushed the envelope, trying to get their planes into "friendly" territory. Within five minutes, all the planes in the West Texas sectors under Kiss's control were cleared from the sky. The traffic situation display equipment, normally showing all the planes flying in a sector of airspace, went totally blank. He stared at it for a moment. How eerie it was to see a blank screen in a facility that is normally operational seven days a week, twenty-four hours a day.

Finally able to let down the professional demeanor that came with the job, Kiss went to the facility's break room to look at the events occurring far away from Texas. Horrified, he thought, "It couldn't be happening!" The replays showed the towers falling and his heart went with them. Texas seemed a long way from the Pentagon and New York City, but when it's your country under attack, distance no longer exists.

Four minutes before the first plane hit the north tower of the World Trade Center, forty-five people on United Airlines flight 93 (UA93) took off from Newark, New Jersey, leaving terminal A, Gate 17, at 8:42am, nearly three-quarters of an hour late due to congestion in the airways, winging their way to San Francisco. The flight headed toward the Cleveland ARTCC at 30,000 feet, while the pilots listened to the instructions of the controllers. The cockpit crew, pilot Captain Jason Dahl and first officer Leroy Homer, had already been warned through a company communication system that another United airplane had been hijacked. At 9:28am a burst of activity came onto the air-traffic control frequency. An utterance of surprise, muffled yells, and an exclamation like, "Hey, get out of here!" Silence for many seconds. Then another voice, not recognized as one of the pilot's, spit out something unintelligible to the listening controllers. Reportedly both of the cockpit crew were severely injured or killed during the assault on the cockpit while another passenger already lay on the floor, murdered. The controllers called Captain Dahl trying to get him to confirm his altitude. As they waited for a response, they heard another odd announcement in an accented voice, "This is your captain speaking. Remain in your seat. Stay quiet. We are returning to the airport." [6]

The hijackers herded almost all the passengers of UA93 to the rear of the 757-200 airplane, where many risked retribution by making calls on cell phones. Flight attendant Sandra Bradshaw contacted her husband while Todd Beamer used a back-of-the-seat phone to connect with the GTE-Verizon switchboard. They both shared the unfolding tale to these listeners. Beamer had been scheduled on a Monday flight, but decided to spend one more day home with his family and rebooked the Tuesday flight. Thomas Burnett, Jr. called his wife in San Ramon, California.

At 9:38am controllers at Cleveland ARTCC noticed the plane as it turned south, but bomb threats called in concerning four other planes focused their attention onto what they believed to be more critical maneuvers. Moments later, the transponder on UA93 was turned off, leaving the controllers without any target on their scopes. The transponder signature on the screen faded. By the time the controllers looked again, the plane had disappeared. Fearing a crash, the controllers reported it to the supervisors. There was no crash—the giant craft moved almost directly over the Pittsburgh air-traffic control tower, angling southeast toward Washington, D.C. The control tower reported through a communications hookup with the Regional Office that they had a rogue plane on their radars, but that it was not squawking the hijack code. As the jumbo jet raced closer to the tower at an alarmingly low altitude, the controllers in the tower were given permission to leave. Several moved toward the exits as others volunteered to stay and track the plane. They watched the blip move south, going faster with each radar sweep.

Controllers at the Cleveland ARTCC had by now identified the correct blip on their screens and were momentarily heartened when the transponder suddenly began transmitting again between altitudes of 6,400 and 5,900. Then the data block disappeared. The controllers and managers in the New York ARTCC could also see the plane on their scopes—it was at the limits of their ability to distinguish with the current radar configuration, but it was discernable. Mike McCormick knew without question that this was number four in a series of attacks. He had seen the radar images of all of the doomed planes and once again agonized. He could do nothing to protect the people of Washington, D.C., clearly where the plane was headed. McCormick watched the screen as each radar sweep announced the rapid descent of the jet. It went downward until it reached 13,000 feet, the lower limits of the radar's capability, beyond which the people in the New York facility could no longer track. Hours would pass before they learned the final story of the passengers aboard UA93.

Inside the runaway jet, as it moved south toward an unknown destination, the callers learned of the other crashes. They realized they were a part of the larger and more deadly dance of death. The UA93 pilots had been killed in an awful and violent attack on the cockpit. The controllers heard the mayhem as the pilot left the microphone keyed open when the attack began. Moments ticked by. The plane continued to race south. Instead of allowing their airplane to complete its deadly mission, the passengers courageously decided to try retaking control of the plane. From the back of the airplane with several armed hijackers between them and the cockpit, this was going to be a difficult battle. Reports came in cell phone calls of preparation of boiling water to be used as a weapon. Wine bottles might also have been pressed into service as clubs. Several of the male passengers, young, fit men strenuously objected to their plane being used as a missile to kill other innocent people. With these few, pitiful weapons, a group of the passengers charged up the center aisle of the plane. A fierce struggle ensued as the passengers tried to wrest flight 93 from the hijackers.

Finally having caught up on the learning curve of events happening on this awful morning, nearby, a fighter jet was positioning itself between UA93 and the District of Columbia. There would be no more buildings attacked today. The pilot of a general aviation plane, requested to look for the United flight as it flew through the Pennsylvania countryside, spotted the jetliner, reporting that it was moving fast and low toward the south. The jumbo jet began darting erratically over the sky—maybe the unskilled terrorist pilot was having difficulty flying the plane or maybe the attack was verging on being successful. Radio transmissions contained voices seconds before the silence, of a man (assumed a hijacker) yelling,

"Get out of here. Get out of here." [7] Sounds of a scuffle ensued. An unofficial version of the information contained on the flight voice recorder "black box," indicates the passengers fought their way into the cockpit using a rolling cart like the ones utilized to serve drinks. But they never regained positive control and the plane dove toward the ground, crashing in a field southwest of Pittsburgh, near Shanksville, Pennsylvania. The plane came toward the ground almost vertical at well over 500 miles per hour, creating only a 30x50 foot crater in the countryside. It was carrying an almost full complement of jet fuel, crashing with such force that it disintegrated into pieces no larger than the palm of one's hand. Everyone on board was killed in this small deep crater as the fireball rolled upward toward the sky. It crashed only thirty minutes flying time from downtown Washington. The general aviation pilot still hovering nearby reported seeing a puff of smoke. It was 10:10am.

Experienced FAA managers, who have served both as controllers and pilots, who heard the cockpit tapes believe that if the plane had been flying at a higher altitude when the passenger rebellion occurred it might have been successful.

Later that morning, jumpy observers reported an airplane crash at Camp David, Maryland, the weekend sanctuary of the U.S. President. The FAA called the military to confirm the crash and was reassured that no crash had occurred at the presidential retreat.

By now, most of the FAA "family" was experiencing emotions ranging from frustration to despair, helplessness, and anger. Eastern region's Hatfield said, "Things could not have been worse." This very large, but extremely close-knit group of people, some of whom were second- or third-generation FAA employees, were used to contributing to and supporting a system that kept everything in control. Today ninety-nine percent of the airplanes were in control, but that one percent over which they had no say was causing the people to react in an unusual way. For the family to have four crashes occur on a single day could not have been any worse.

Later, Attorney General John Ashcroft confirmed that UA93 was most likely headed for a major target in Washington. "Our government has credible evidence that the White House and Air Force One were targets," he said. [8] Others thought that the target was the Capitol or Camp David. Months later a captured member of the terrorist organization al Qaeda confirmed that to his knowledge the White House was the target.

By now, both towers of the World Trade Center had imploded in a mind-numbing cascade of Volkswagen-sized chunks of concrete, steel, and glass. Thousands were trapped and killed instantly. The south tower had fallen at 9:51am, the north a little over a half an hour later, at 10:28am.

The Pentagon, in clear view from several FAA and other downtown offices gushed smoke—thick and black—helped along by thousands of gallons of jet fuel. The plane had vaporized large parts of the west wall. Coincidentally, exactly sixty years before the attack on the Pentagon, on September 11, 1941, the groundbreaking ceremony had been held for this behemoth. It was a record-sized building created in an effort to consolidate all the defense operations functioning throughout the Washington area. In the months after the first shovels of dirt were turned, over 10,000 people worked on the building. After Pearl Harbor, the three-story building was redesigned to be five stories tall. Concrete ramps took the place of elevators and all the walls were made of reinforced concrete. In under a year and a half, the five-sided building was completed. Its halls totaled nearly twenty miles, with an area of 6,500,000 square feet. Five different five-story buildings placed parallel to each other in concentric circles, connected with crossing halls make up each side of the building. They are called rings.

AA77 managed to penetrate three of the five rings, initially leaving a tunnel through the exterior wall into the other rings. Then as fire ate away supporting members of the building, it collapsed into a crush of cement and flames creating a rescuer's nightmare. The fourth ring, the next to the last one toward the interior, had a hole smashed through it from the force of the explosion, which fortuitously became an escape route for many of the survivors fleeing from the damage in the other three rings. A monstrous gash was visible in the outer ring. The wreckage was so complete, that even six weeks later it was a devastating sight to view. Jagged concrete and rebar hung down into the wound. Black burn marks rose up the stone of those walls still standing, showing the awful heat trail as the smoke made its way out of the building. Windows with two-inch thick security "glass" shattered and smoke marked the stone around each of them as well. Casualties would have been much greater without these newly installed security windows. Thick and impact resistant, they shielded many from the initial blast of burning fuel and debris. A marine officer, standing two windows away from the impact area, sheltered by one of the windows, was unscathed after the crash and managed to escape.

The hijacker's choice of the southwest perimeter was also fortuitous in that this entire area had been under refurbishment for months. Construction crews had recently completed installation of the hardening measures and federal and contract personnel had only within the last few days begun repopulating the area. If these measures had not been between the plane and the people and had there been the normal contingent of workers in the area, hundreds more people would have died.

Miraculously, a twenty-three-person contract crew, installing building furniture in the exact area of impact, had just evacuated that section of the building. As the trauma in New York City was airing on CNN, a crewmember's wife phoned her husband reporting a feeling that he was in danger at the Pentagon. After hearing of the first attacks, the crew leader instructed all twenty-three workers to abandon their tools and quickly leave the building. Moments after clearing the building's confines, as they ran across the parking lot, the crew was shocked to see the airliner bury itself into the section they had just deserted.

Despite the sturdiness, the twenty-nine acre, internationally known landmark took quite a beating. In all 400,000 square feet of the one million square foot section of the building, through all five floors of three rings, were damaged severely enough to require demolition and rebuilding. Rescue efforts began immediately. Then recovery efforts followed for several days. This task continued for twenty-four hours a day, seven days a week, desperately looking for survivors at first, finally trying to find all the remains for the waiting families.

For many bystanders, the most mentally devastating part of viewing the damage was the realization of the extent of the force created by the impact of the airliner and the immediate obliteration of all organisms on and around the plane. Most of all, the gash in the building was personal—the damage almost a physical wound. The attack went to the core of the country's being. The Pentagon represents the nation's pride—built in the midst of another nationally trying time—emblematic of strength and service to this nation and others world wide.

As the search and rescue mission was completed, design work to repair the national headquarters began straight away. The engineers had no time to redesign the building, so they used the sixty-year-old original drawings to reconstruct the broken section. New innovations were included, affording even greater protections than before. Kevlar coverings, already being used in the refurbished section, were replaced to strengthen each wall. The safety windows, responsible for saving so many lives during the attack, were replaced and added to other sections as well. Combined with other security and safety innovations, the Pentagon will be a sanctuary again. Since the building is a National Registered Landmark, extraordinary care had to be taken to ensure that the outside appearance was not altered. The replaced windows were fashioned to look like the initial ones—fake handles were attached, mirroring the originals that had opened to the outside when needed. False screen slides were molded into the sides of each window, preserving the original look as well.

The new granite used to rebuild the outside of the facility was quarried near the original 1940s quarry site in Indiana. Inside the upgraded section of the five-sided building, in the escalator bay, imbedded in one of the knee walls is a very special piece of the mined stone. Hammered into the stone countenance facing the public, to everyone who glances its way is a quote from President Bush: "Terrorist acts can shake the foundations of our biggest building, but cannot touch the foundation of America." Etched around the quote are the signatures of quarry personnel, intent on showing their support to the Pentagon personnel during the days of darkness. Secretary of Defense Rumsfeld promised that the damage would be repaired within a year. In fact, it was re-inhabited several weeks before the first anniversary of the attack.

5

Even as air traffic was being halted on Tuesday morning, federal employees were reacting nationwide. In places as far away as Florida's Kennedy Space Center, with the shuttle fleet in residence, the facility was put on its highest alert for the first time ever. Everyone but a skeleton crew was sent home; those left rode out the next several hours in the emergency operations center. Helicopters buzzed overhead ensuring that the area was secure from terror. American embassies were closed throughout the world, while border crossings were locked down all around the country. Major western dams were closed to all visitors and guarded very closely from the sky.

The Office of Personnel Management ordered an evacuation from their office buildings of all federal personnel nationwide at 10:08am. The threat of another attack of some sort on the capital city demanded all the potential targets in Washington be emptied of human cargo. People poured out of buildings onto the streets of Washington and began walking—some to the subway, some to carpools—others who had given up trying to find transportation began trudging toward home. Traffic was immediately gridlocked into a mess of metal spaghetti frozen into place at every intersection and tunnel throughout the city. Thousands of people trod the streets, but the quiet was deafening. They walked, slowly, deliberately, almost with no direction. Shock was the only emotion registering. Their faces, identical by the hundreds, had a far-away look seen only in movies depicting nuclear survivors. In the quiet, an odd sound compelled everyone to look upward—fighter aircraft flew station over the nation's capital. No one could remember a time when this had happened. No one could decide if it made him feel better or worse.

Things moved fast above the city. After the Pentagon attack, the Secret Service called near-by Andrews Air Force Base, asking them to send up fighters to protect the city from another likely assault. The only thing the brass at Andrews had to send up were planes from the 121st Fighter Squadron—the District of Columbia Air National Guard. They swept into the air—four F-16s ready to defend the District at all costs. The pilots could see the flaming Pentagon building as they became airborne. Because they weren't using a common frequency, they had no idea other fighters were in the area (F-16s from Langley Air Force Base), making mass confusion for the air-traffic controllers. Fighters from Richmond and Atlantic City soon joined the mix, muddling things even more. Controllers were trying to land all commercial planes while also vectoring the myriad fighters toward any unidentified craft that might be posing a threat to the city. "The FAA controllers were doing their best to get us information," the pilots reported. But, without having the AWACS with which the fighter pilots were used to working, instructions became garbled. Normal navigation procedures were abandoned and, "Eventually, Washington Reagan National Airport was designated 'Bullseye,' and fighters were given range and bearing to targets from there." [1]

As most federal workers filed out in response to the evacuation order, others settled into the buildings, making the government ready for whatever was to come next. FAA investigations manager Dave Canoles' mind registered one thought. "We might be at war by afternoon." [2] Those who stayed in the buildings were the people responsible for making the nation function in times of emergencies. They don't get to go home to see to the safety of their families. Filled with these kinds of people, the FAA building was alive with action. They had all manned their battle stations.

Planning and Procedures Program Special Operations Division member Rick Hostetler, on his way from an aborted root canal, had been unable to find a way from his location in Waldorf, Maryland into Northern Virginia that wasn't completely blocked by stalled traffic. He had initially tried to use Washington's infamous Beltway to transit over the Wilson Bridge, to no avail. He wheeled his car in the opposite direction, leaving the Beltway and moved north, using Maryland's Route 301. He finally hooked up onto southbound Interstate 95 and was able to get past downtown Washington to his destination. But it had taken him hours. By this time, he had heard of all the attacks through his beeper, cell phone, and the car radio and began planning for the post-attack contingency issues he knew would greet him at the door of the Command Center. His first task was to coordinate with his Pentagon counterpart and determine the locations of every major government leader. He, like many others, began watching for any signs indicating a second wave of attacks.

Mike McCormick, New York ARTCC manager, called his wife, requesting she bring him some clothes and a blanket. He knew that he wasn't going home for several days. The same scenario was playing out at dozens of other FAA facilities, nationwide.

Tony Ferrante, manager of the FAA's investigations arm, had confirmed that he was stuck in Chicago for the duration. He became increasingly uncomfortable with this quarantine, knowing that he should be one of those people at his post in

Washington, D.C. If there, he knew he could begin gathering the forensic data that would give some of the answers about the hijackings and the crashes. His first and foremost concern was determining how the air-traffic control system personnel, procedures, and equipment had performed during and after the crisis. He had already been told by the FAA's Great Lakes Regional management that an attempt to rent a car for him to use to hurry back to Washington had been rebuffed by the rental companies. His cell phone was useless, because it was calibrated to a Washington, D.C. exchange and those circuits had been jammed from the first hit in New York City.

Faced with having to stay in Chicago for an undetermined length of time, he finally borrowed a federally owned van and a Chicago cell phone and began determinedly driving the 700-mile trip toward the FAA headquarters. He raced as fast as he safely could, hoping that a vehicle with a government license plate and his Department of Transportation identification card would fend off most speeding tickets. With the quiet of the road came a million different thoughts flooding into his consciousness. Only the radio and an occasional chirping of the Chicago cell phone broke his thought patterns as he went over the events. Different worries kept chasing themselves through his mind unbidden, like enraged hamsters on a running wheel. What kinds of qualifications did these people have? It wasn't easy to fly into those three buildings at 500 miles an hour—how did they do it, were they pilots? Where is my son? Did he get home from school okay?

As the hours and the miles passed and day turned to night, additional information was relayed through the van's radio, tuned to local stations, or from intermittent phone calls from headquarters. His wife called several times, checking on him, making sure he didn't fall asleep at the wheel. After an excruciating twelve hours on the highway, he pulled into his driveway in Northern Virginia at 1:00am on Wednesday.

Hundreds of the people working through the night in the FAA headquarters building reflected that only a week ago, a day ago, an hour ago, the most pressing issue for the FAA was finding new innovations that would stretch the capacity of a very popular system. On August 2, 2001, Administrator Garvey, in testimony to the Congressional Subcommittee on Transportation and Related Agencies, had been upbeat on the capacity problems. "We are making real measurable progress on delays. The Department and the FAA are aggressively moving major new runway projects through the environmental review pipeline." [3] Now another perspective was in order.

The air-traffic control system is an intricate combination of equipment, software, processes, and people. Through a series of controllers, radars, communication, and navigation equipment, 35,000 planes are moved across the sky each day allowing 1.9 million people to go about their business. Up until 8:46am on September 11, the system was being overwhelmed by too many people, wanting to go too many places, too often. No longer. The only problem later that day was safety and security. Now with a new outlook, acting Deputy Administrator Monte Belger would testify to congress on September 25: "Given the events of last week, assumptions underlying aviation security have fundamentally changed." [4] No one knew at this point what the new reality was going to be, but everyone braced for significant, necessary changes.

Wilbur and Orville Wright fledged the entire industry on a windy dune at Kitty Hawk, North Carolina, in 1903 and in less than twenty-three years an entire federal regulating organization was created to organize and protect what was to become one of the most important industries in the world. Initially, the Air Commerce Act of 1926 had mandated what would become a long trail of federal regulation in aviation with safety benefiting most of all. The industry had spent the twenty years previous to that as a rollicking, barnstorming circus used as entertainment more than anything else. As a transportation method for people, it had been loathe to catch on, but as a mail carrying system, it immediately became popular and ultimately critical to the nation, explaining why it was originally regulated in the Department of Commerce.

Regulation came haltingly because the brand new field of aviation had been the playground of the mavericks and entrepreneurs who felt that government regulation would tame it too much. In the formative years, commercial airlines were in many aspects similar to utilities and regulated in a like manner. As with many new industries, the aviation trade was not thrilled by any discipline, especially on a federal level. But a new world had blossomed sometime between the Wright brothers and the space age, creating a vast new frontier of economic possibilities that required a corresponding response from the aviation managers in Washington. Inevitably, people who had until now flown when, where, and how they liked proved difficult to rein in. These were people who were used to succeeding by the sweat of their own brows in an era of rural dominance in the U.S.

Mostly agrarian, time and space in the U.S. were almost insurmountable—until the airplane made spanning the nation an endeavor of hours instead of days. In an era of parallel productivity, sometimes compared with the last decade of the Twentieth Century, prosperity was considered a birthright and was enjoyed by an entire nation. A mantra of materialism ensued. The FAA chronicle, *Bonfires to Beacons* quoted Robert L. Heilbroner who said, "'The country was drunk with the elixir of prosperity.' Some men believed the good times would never end and poverty would become only a dim reminder of a cruel and unenlightened past." [5] The airplane served as a tool for this prosperity and to have its wings clipped by federal rules for safety's sake rubbed many of them the wrong way—even if it was for their own health and well-being.

Ultimately, all involved seemed to understand that the business was too big for private industry to manage. Thus was born the symbiotic relationship that more or less exists today between the government, commercial industry, and general aviation—a pact whereby the government regulates the business of airplanes so that not only is safety a by-product, but profit is also another of the primary outcomes.

While air passenger service officially began a few days after the law was signed in May 1926, the initial impetus for regulated air traffic was to support the movement of the United States mail—a sort of airborne Pony Express. A one-way passenger trip from Washington, D.C. to Philadelphia cost fifteen dollars. At those prices and with only two or three passengers per trip, the mail truly paid the way for many of the airlines to become the multi-billion dollar business they are today. Northwest Airlines began service in 1926 as a mail carrier and then evolved into a passenger business. Pan American Airways also began during the dawning of the industry.

In support of both the safety and economic needs of the brand new industry, an early navigation system was established, including a light beacon system that began operation on December 7, 1926. The initial course covered with beacons was used on the Chicago-Dallas mail route. So significant was this new innovation to mail delivery that within six months, over four thousand miles of lighted navigable airways criss-crossed the country. One of the intrepid pilots whose job it was to deliver the mail was none other than Charles Lindbergh.

In slightly more than a decade, the Air Commerce Act had given way to the Civil Aeronautics Act of 1938, which created the Civil Aeronautics Authority (CAA). Still burdened with the duty of regulating safety, the act also deepened the role of economic regulation. It was broken into three distinct regulating positions. The five-member board of the Civil Aeronautics Authority (a subset of the larger organization named the same) was responsible for the safety and economic regulation; the Administrator of the Authority was the day-to-day operational manager of the agency; and the Air Safety Board was responsible for accident investigations. New laws applied to items such as airmail rates, passenger rates, and the business practices of the airlines.

Transferring the agency from being a mere branch of the Commerce Department to its own organization at the behest of the 1938 bill was both brilliant and damaging—asking a single agency to both be the watchdog and the cheerleader of a single industry from then till now has created a lasting and antagonistic psychology, but it has also demanded a fine touch, not heavy to either issue, creating an almost perfect balance.

Turmoil marked the CAA from the beginning as it struggled to become a true federal regulating authority. Made up of the "...safety and airway regulation from the Bureau of Air Commerce, the mail rate setting from the Interstate Commerce Commission, and route and schedule control from the Post Office Department," [6] it spent years searching for an identity. Certification of pilots and mechanics quickly became a focus of the CAA as it tried to ensure the safety of the flying public. Airworthiness of aircraft was looked into, as were the production processes of each type of aircraft. And they had to do all of this without squashing the nascent economic strugglings of the industry as it sought a niche in the nation's daily economy.

Conflict-of-interest pressures on the Commerce Department and subsequently the CAA also cropped up, as inevitably crashes occurred, bringing with each a litany of death and destruction. As each accident was investigated and reported upon, the federal aviation entity was a party of interest in all the crashes, and constantly at odds with itself in dealing with both safety and economics. A May 6, 1935 crash that killed Senator Bronson Cutting brought the issues into sharp focus. TWA, owner of the crashed airplane, and the federal government engaged in a fierce battle of blame. The president of the airline asked: "Can a Government agency sit in judgment upon an activity in which it itself participates?" [7]

Throughout its existence budget battles ensued with every incarnation of the FAA losing at almost every turn. With each advance, technology has inspired the FAA to improve many of its systems with state-of-the-art equipment. Funding has pressured them to do it slowly because, within the executive branch of the federal system, the FAA has often lost out on the budget battles on Capitol Hill.

In the early CAA days, infighting in the administration often served only to alienate Congress and tighten the purse strings. The federal government was slow in recognizing the importance of aviation on the health of the nation, so little significant budget was invested in the nation's newest industry with only a few projects being attempted prior to 1939. Finally, realizing that the country was far behind in answering the need of the populace, by May 1, 1939, the CAA had completed a $7 million modernization program, including the upgrading of communications, navigation, and landing facilities.

The request to Congress for the 1940 appropriation was approximately $35 million, but the administration only managed to wring $23.2 million out of an offended budget director. By now, the funding requirements of the CAA were growing more rapidly than Congress could see to provide for. Regulations proliferated and the budget to support them was not forthcoming. The new authority was responsible for regulating airmail rates, airline rates, fares, routes, and the business practices of the airline companies themselves. Additionally, the organization was supposed to establish civil airways, provide and establish air-navigation facilities, and support the development of airports and airways. All in all, it was a giant job thrust onto an organization that was woefully unprepared for it. Without the needed funding support from Congress, no chance existed for the CAA to be successful.

The war clouds in the early 1940s forced a reassessment of priorities and a massive infrastructure development effort was begun, building airports and training pilots. Through this program many pilots were first trained, creating an initial cadre of flyers when needed at the beginning of the war. The 1941 budget more than quadrupled from the previous year with a final appropriation of $103.4 million.

Funding subsequently ballooned and contracted depending on the events shaping the nation and the world. Financial levels rose until in 1948, at $119 million, the level retreated to a peacetime level that was two million less than that of 1947. By 1950 a record $207 million was handed to the CAA. The agency used this money just trying to keep up with the swift advances happening not only in the industry, but also in the country's emerging position as a world leader. Just as the administration was beginning to gain steam, the Korean War trimmed the budget of almost every non-war-related organization in the government. The 1951 budget was $231 million but lost nearly twenty million midyear when the war began. Shrinking still, the 1952 budget of $155 million was a shocking amount compared to the hey days of 1950 and 1951. At $141 million in 1953, the CAA seemed to be shrinking. At its lowest level since the 1940s, the 1954 budget, supported by the Eisenhower administration, was a mere $116 million achieved by cutting 1,500 positions, shutting down control tower operations at some airports, and minimizing services to the general aviation community. Hardly the indication of a burgeoning industry.

Years of regulation barely kept pace, and in some cases did not keep up with an industry that was annually growing by leaps and bounds. The infrastructure was inadequate, causing noted aviation expert and later FAA administrator, Najeeb Halaby, to say on June 25, 1955, "We have now a situation where every time any one of us either flies his own airplane or gets on an airline, he is going into an air situation that is inefficiently instrumented and controlled and so he is often late or directed to another field or cannot take off simply because the CAA, realizing the inadequacy of the system, must straitjacket the traffic." [8]

In most cases, the budget process responded to crises in the industry. "When a rash of accidents took place, the agency came under intense scrutiny. Congress and the White House would conduct investigations and feverishly formulate recommendations. Then, often just as quickly, normality would return. For the CAA, that generally meant a return to laboring in obscurity—trying to pry loose more money for navigation aids while carrying on its exacting regulatory activities and a limited research program." [9] Just such a rash of accidents hit the CAA in 1947. In a May 29 accident at LaGuardia Airport, the combination of an overloaded airplane and high winds caused a crash resulting in the death of thirty-eight people. Close on its heels another crash, the next day killed fifty-three people, and weeks later on June 13, fifty more people died when the airplane flew into the Blue Ridge Mountains in bad weather. While all the accidents were billed as airline problems, a subsequent accident report chastised Congress for "...penny-pinching on landing aids for which the legislators had provided only four percent of the funds and facilities requested for 1948." [10]

Another series of crashes pummeled the country and the industry in 1951 when, once again, in a matter of weeks a frightening number of lives were lost. Beginning December 16, 1951 when a C-46 crashed after leaving Newark Airport, until April 1952 an incredible four crashes occurred, leaving hundreds dead in accidents that happened in the air as well as on the ground. One of the four mishaps involved a plane full of people that in late January hit a six-story building in Elizabeth, New Jersey, killing twenty-three in the air and six on the ground. As airline response and airport safety was raked over the coals again, the penury of Congress was cited as having created the problem after not having funded clear areas at the ends of all the runways at major airports.

Even after the notorious Grand Canyon crash of 1956 when it became obvious that additional air traffic control was needed, Congress was reluctant to take up the issue. A CAA supplemental request for $68 million was scorned to the point that ultimately Congress wound up cutting $23 million from the bottom line before agreeing to it. The industry recognized the amount as short sighted and dangerous. FAA history book *Take-off at Mid-Century* quotes the periodical *Aviation Week* as being fit to be tied and using its editorial pages to excoriate "the

84th Congress's 'sorry, shameful record' and 'calloused attitude,' characterizing a congressional committee's junket to inspect the Grand Canyon accident scene as 'a gay weekend in Las Vegas at the taxpayers' expense." [(11)]

More recently, from 1992 until 2000 the FAA budget mostly retreated in the face of more pressing needs from other of the nation's constituencies. Much of the budget emanates from the FAA's Trust Fund—a federal tax fund designed to fence off income from the aviation industry for use by the FAA—which has been a controversial issue in itself.

Most of the trepidation with which the nation regards the FAA's budget seems to revolve around the uneasy alliance between industry and government. Foremost in many people's minds is that any budget upgrades seem to support only a small portion of the population, but most people seem clueless as to the impacts of the aviation industry. Millions upon millions of jobs are reliant upon a healthy flying industry and millions more businesses rely upon the daily products of the aviation industry…mail and freight movement, postal service, and the banking industry to name a few.

Massive improvements were critical in ensuring that significant numbers of flights served the nation each day. Despite the improvements, in what was to become a cyclical and never-ending problem, as a mid-century modernization effort was completed, it became apparent that the airports were creating both a bottleneck and a capacity issue. FAA history book, *Turbulence Aloft* stated, "More serious was the shortage of airports and the limited bad-weather capacity of those that existed." [(12)] Obvious to even the most casual observer, it became a cycle that would be repeated many times. Too many flights were needed to meet demand and runways, airports, and weather technology were hindering many of those flights.

In an eerie *deja vue* with the modern-day aviation system—capacity has recently been overwhelmed by the continued popularity of cheap and available air travel. From nothing at the beginning of the Twentieth Century to the transportation of 1.5 billion passengers a year at the beginning of the Twenty-first Century, there was simply too much of a good thing. Until September 11, 2001, continual bad news in the form of capacity problems dogged the FAA's administrator and deputy administrator, daily. An overwhelming number of flights were late in either taking off or landing, or in some cases, both. Additional flights during peak hours were impossible, leaving paying passengers without sufficient airplane seats. The airlines were losing money and the system was becoming clogged.

Previously, bad news came in the form of accidents, which everyone in the system worked intently to prevent. No system is perfect and recognition of these realities were often left unspoken in the formative years of the industry, but as Jerome Lederer of the Flight Safety Foundation said in 1956, "No greater evil could befall aviation than a fatal collision between two large air transport." [13] The Grand Canyon accident on June 30 1956 was the awful denial to his unspoken prayer. Two large passenger jets stumbled into each other at about 21,000 feet in uncontrolled airspace near the Grand Canyon, crashing to the brown desert ground below, leaving scars on the countryside that were difficult for the nation to erase from its mind. Between 1950 and 1955, sixty-five midair collisions happened in the United States, mostly because of congestion. Earlier, in 1955, horror of a deliberate kind had been visited onto the aviation industry for what was probably the first time in the United States, but as was proven on September 11, 2001 not the last. A United Airlines flight took off from Denver on November 1, 1955 and minutes later was blown apart by a bomb that killed all forty-four people on board. At the bottom of the bombing was a man whose mother, a passenger on the plane, had a very large insurance policy.

Despite a rugged beginning, the CAA as the regulating organization of aviation mostly fulfilled its role. A changing world forced the United States to consider the security of the aviation industry as a whole. Early in 1948, a report called *Survival in the Air Age* was published. For what was probably the first time, international dangers to the industry were outlined. "The range of modern airplanes and the development of atomic weapons…forced a fundamental rethinking of the traditional American assumption that the oceans provided a secure buffer behind which the nation could mobilize its huge industrial capacity. Such a major readjustment in American thinking would not be easy, as it was far simpler for a totalitarian nation than for a democracy to arm to the hilt in peacetime." [14] Despite these early words, it would be fifty-three more years before the oceans would be breached.

The CAA, from almost its inception, spent a great deal of time and money spreading its vast wealth of knowledge to other countries. In an odd historical footnote, on September 27, 1956, aviation specialists from the CAA formed a team to support Afghanistan by providing technical assistance in creating a national airways system. In order to expand the country's system, personnel and $14,560,000 were loaned to support the effort. Some of the still-existing infrastructure of that country's aviation system, things from which the al Qaeda terrorists benefited, is the result of that initial loan of funding and knowledge by the United States.

On August 23, 1958, the Federal Aviation Act divested much of the structure created in 1926 and 1938 and fashioned one new agency and changed the mission of another. Morphed from the Civil Aeronautics Administration, the Airways Modernization Board, and parts of the Civil Aeronautics Board (CAB), the FAA as we know it today was created as an independent agency by the Federal Aviation Act of 1958.

The Federal Aviation Agency (later changed to Administration) was created as a safety and regulatory organization, while the CAB was streamlined into an entity that was almost exclusively interested in the economic regulation of the aviation industry. It was an attempt to separate the two competing mandates of the agency—safety and economic viability—and give distinct, non-competing roles to two different organizations.

At the domestic high point of the Eisenhower presidency, with this act came the centralization of power, creating an FAA that took on a completely new persona. It was a violent coming of age. The outcome of its creation was likened to the convergence of two weather fronts. "After many years of relatively weak regulation, the civil aviation community was like a hot air mass filled with fears about the loss of freedom. Quesada, [the first FAA administrator] with his belief in a strong regulatory role for FAA, was like a cold polar air mass. When the two fronts collided, a violent storm complete with thunder and lightning broke out." (15)

Despite the ferocious beginning of the agency, it evolved and for years regulated only commercial airline routes, safety, and certification of aircraft and various personnel. Fares continued to be the province of the Civil Aeronautics Board. As the free-market concept strengthened in the nation, it became obvious that fare management was not creating the best economic outcome for the airlines. In 1978, the Civil Aeronautics Board gave up its last responsibility: the cost structures were deregulated, allowing the industry to regulate itself based on supply and demand. Often recognized as a masterful economic move, deregulation has made an impossible job even harder for the FAA. Deregulation brought immediate pressure on every airline to lower the price of each seat to be competitive with its fellow airlines. Lower prices demanded lower overheads in the companies, tempting many to consider changing their maintenance support structure. Safety against cost. But lower costs also brought a huge influx of passengers, creating a demand for far more service than the industry and the FAA had to offer.

The FAA employs about 50,000 people. Despite being labeled with the all-encompassing epithet of "bureaucrat," each one of these people has a face, and a family, and aspirations to do well. Daily dedication of FAA employees is well known among the ranks of that organization. Being good neighbors is part of the package.

One evening several years ago in a small town in Alaska, the local infirmary suddenly became inadequate to treat the severe illness of a local patient. Without more sophisticated treatment the patient would die. The airport had no landing lights or controller on duty after dusk, thus was inaccessible after dark. An emergency ambulance flight was called, while residents of the town lined the runway with their cars. The airport was reopened and an air-traffic controller quickly pressed into service guided the emergency flight downward toward a runway that was now illuminated by the lights of Chevrolets and Buicks. Safely down, the patient was loaded and the controller sent the plane on its way.

Across the continent, members of another section of the FAA were torn when one of their own was almost fatally injured. Embry-Riddle Aeronautical University senior Lourdes Sanabria was hired as a safety clerk at the Flight Standards District Office (FSDO) in Miami, Florida. Within months of starting her new job, Sanabria was severely injured in an auto crash. After experiencing a three-month coma, she spent the next twenty-one months recovering in the hospital. Sanabria had no leave time and was in danger of not being paid. Her fellow employees came to her aid. During all her time away from the job, a paycheck showed up in her mailbox each month because "...FAA employees from all over the country donated more than 4,000 hours of leave," sustaining her through her trauma. [16] FAA personnel from Alaska, California, New York, Texas, and at overseas stations donated leave for her until months later she returned to work. But even getting to work was an almost insurmountable issue. Sanabria cannot walk due to permanent injuries from the accident, so her mobility and commuting predicament have became almost overwhelming. Today, Lourdes's FAA co-workers are devising unusual fund-raising methods to help her buy specialized transportation with a wheelchair lift so she'll be able to commute to work with ease.

When severe windstorms damaged a critical radar at Boston's Logan Airport at the beginning of the Easter holiday, April 2000, it looked as though this major airport would have to be closed for days or maybe even weeks until the radar could be replaced. Shutting down the ninth busiest airport in the United States and major player in the East Coast corridor created a massive groundswell of schedule damage throughout the country and was keeping many passengers from traveling on a holiday. International flights were affected, as were the thousands of domestic flights that normally landed and departed from there. The equipment was totaled and the New England regional air-traffic facilities manager,

John Zalenchak, noted, "In essence we were faced with building a new radar system from the ground up." [17] This job normally took months of planning and execution.

A team of technicians and managers met, quickly sketching out a solution. The military was called and finagled into providing air transport for new parts. Radars of this type are not stockpiled, so the only possible set of spares in the entire inventory was located at the FAA's Aeronautical Center in Oklahoma City. Parts were scavenged from test and training equipment as well as pulled from the regular inventory of replacement parts kept at the huge facility. In something less than a day, all the parts had been found and put into operational order by technicians who worked throughout the holiday, trying to restore service to Logan Airport. A C-17 transport plane borrowed from the U.S. Air Force was packed full of equipment including a 5-ton antenna array and raced to Boston from Oklahoma. Over the next two days of Easter weekend, a team of specialists—from Oklahoma City, New England Region, and Boston Airport—installed the radar, tested it, and within a matter of days did what it would have ordinarily taken several months to accomplish. They worked without rest for almost three days in the cold, with a constant driving rain creating miserable working conditions.

Others members of the FAA family have worked through days and nights restoring equipment to working condition after the onslaught of devastating hurricanes. As soon as the winds die down in the affected area, teams of technicians begin sweeping the countryside assessing damage done to the wide array of the FAA's navigation and communications suite of equipment. After Hurricane Andrew, a team based in the Southern Region was notified of severe damage to essential equipment. The team loaded their repair tools into a service van and went to work. They were on the road repairing various systems for days, but because of the severe damage done to local businesses, they had no hotels to which to retire each night. They slept in the van and showered in the local state armory for days until the job was complete.

6

Shortly before 9:00am on September 11, 2001, the air-traffic control system had under positive control 4,546 planes executing their flights under instrument flight rule (IFR). Four were identifiably rogue. Rumors swirled as to others also having been hijacked. At 9:07am a message was sent from the Air Traffic Control System Command Center in northern Virginia to every air traffic facility in the nation, announcing the first hijacking. One minute later at 9:08am a written notice advised all aircraft in the New York airspace to depart or land, thus sterilizing the airspace. Moments later similar commands closed all the airports at Cleveland and Washington, DC. The Boston ARTCC had been closed with a local ground stop order at 9:04am. Airlines began contacting their fleets through company communication networks, advising those on the ground to stay put. In many ways, the nation was lucky that day. Each day as the sun moves across the country's time zones, more and more airplanes take to the skies. Fortunately, because it was still relatively early in the three other time zones spanning the lower forty-eight states, fewer airplanes were airborne than had the hijackings occurred at midday—unfortunately, it was the peak flying time in the Northeast. US Airways had well over two hundred planes in the sky because they mostly service the east coast, but Alaska Airlines had only six flights aloft. As the planes began landing, many had to use runways at airports with which the pilots were not familiar and where the airlines had no landing or servicing agreements. Many of the pilots and copilots were unnerved. Taking off, landing, or waiting was becoming an act of faith written on the airwaves between the managers of the airplanes and the air-traffic controllers.

A copilot, writing anonymously in the December 2001 *Air and Space Magazine*, told of an 8:45am pushback from a gate at Newark Airport and a long wait in the taxi line when suddenly smoke appeared at the World Trade Center, easily visible across the river from the New Jersey airport. "As we taxied south toward runway 4L, we watched the horror unfolding only miles away." Staring at the smoke pouring from Manhattan, they continued to sit in the long line ready for takeoff. Then they were suddenly told by air-traffic control to cut their engines and wait for further orders. Realizing their plane's vulnerability—a long line of large jets just asking to become a target—both the pilot and copilot began plotting an emergency takeoff. "I began to think about the safety of our passengers. I looked over at the captain, 'Do we really want to be sitting here with our engines shut down if New York is under attack?' I asked." They scoped the area for an alternative takeoff plan, noting a smaller crossing runway within reach of their plane. Momentary contemplation was made of overriding the controller's orders with the captain's emergency authority—which reasons that the captain is ultimately responsible for the plane and its passengers and therefore has the final say in the condition of the aircraft—but this thought was discarded because they couldn't guarantee that their plane was free of hijackers. Finally, responding to an air traffic control order, they crept back to the gate, unloading their now stunned, but safe passengers. [1]

Pilots on other planes were also taking stock of their circumstances. United Airlines flight 890, flying from Narita, Japan to Los Angeles had been informed of the attacks through a company cockpit messaging system. The pilot and copilot assessed the slim selection of weapons available to them and decided that blocking the cockpit door and arming one of them with the crash ax was the best they could do. Pilot Jim Hoskings and copilot Doug Price decided to pretend that hijackers were on their plane and planned accordingly. Hoskings tells Price, "If someone tries to come in that door, I don't want you to hurt him. Kill him." [2] Captain Paul Werner, flying Delta flight 1989, was also informed of the attacks while his plane was in the air. In the unique and extremely unenviable position of having the exact profile of the two planes already buried in the World Trade Towers, Delta flight 1989 was a large plane—a Boeing 767—that took off from Boston Logan Airport just minutes after both AA11 and UA175. Werner was okayed to land at Cleveland, but his flight was met by a SWAT team, working on the premise that hijackers might be on board.

Trans-Atlantic flight United 963 was four long hours away from landing when the crew learned of the attacks. Off-duty pilots were summoned to the cockpit and stationed just inside the door with full wine bottles standing ready as weapons. Flight crews on other planes armed themselves with steak knives and used the drink cart as a barrier in front of the door.

At 9:29am all planes on the ground were ordered to stay there. Ground stop! Advisory 031 issued from the FAA's Command Center said:

DUE TO NATIONAL EMERGENCY, GROUND STOP ALL DEPARTURES REGARDLESS OF DESTINATION....REPEAT GROUND STOP ALL DEPARTURES.

Then, a few tense moments later, at 9:45am an order went out commanding all commercial and general aviation planes in the air to land immediately. Advisory 036 also issued from the FAA's Command Center said:

> DUE TO EXTRAORDINARY CIRCUMSTANCESAND FOR REASONS OF SAFETY, ATTENTION ALL AIRCRAFT OPERATORS, BY ORDER OF THE FEDERAL AVIATION COMMAND CENTER ALL AIRPORTS/AIRDROMES ARE NOT AUTHORIZED FOR LANDING AND TAKEOFF. ALL TRAFFIC INCLUDING AIRBORNE AIRCRAFT ARE ENCOURAGED TO LAND SHORTLY, INCLUDING ALL HELICOPTER TRAFFIC. AIRCRAFT INVOLVED IN FIREFIGHTING IN THE NORTHWEST U.S. ARE EXCLUDED.

They were told to find an airport, suitable for their type of aircraft, and land. Many pilots hesitated. They had pressing issues to be considered for their companies—passengers not arriving at their destination as well as landing at airports at which their company had no business contracts. This would hamper returning to the air because refueling and service agreements would not be in place. Reportedly, pilots on a TWA and a US Airways jet were noticeably reluctant and had to be ordered down in no uncertain terms. Understandable, since never subsequent to the time of the Wright Brothers had this order been executed. Not during World War II, not during the Cuban missile crisis, nor during any of the other crises that have gripped the nation has this order ever been given. At 9:45am history was made. Following suit, Transport Canada—Canada's privatized version of the United States' FAA—also ordered a ground stop.

By 10:39am, a formal notice to airmen (NOTAM) was issued shutting down operations at all airports. [3] Air-traffic director Bill Peacock knew in his mind what one of the huge screens located in the control room at the Command Center looked like. It was a map of the United States superimposed with little tiny emblems indicating every plane that was being controlled. He knew that when the ground stop was imposed, around five thousand commercial jets were still up there and had to be kept safely in the air until each was routed downward to the nearest acceptable airport. He worried about all those people up there, the safety of each whom he felt personally responsible. As he and his deputy Jeff Griffith were trying hard to keep their arms around the rapidly moving picture, Peacock thought: now all 5,000 planes have to come down.

A daunting task. But as Peacock explained later, "You don't consider it a 5,000-plane problem." There are twenty-one Air Route Traffic Control Centers as well as numerous other major controlling facilities. Each of those is responsible for a specific portion of airspace at a certain altitude. When the 5,000 aircraft were divided by that many caretakers, suddenly the job was almost manageable. And as Peacock put it, "The system worked just like it's supposed to." Some controllers struggled with the correct procedures for controlling so many airplanes, but ultimately, procedures were met and the descent of all airplanes began in an orderly fashion.

Many others were contemplating the very same image. Administrator Garvey was at the FAA Headquarters Operations Center soon after the attack. As she recalled that morning, her description confirmed what Peacock was imagining. "The strongest image in my mind was watching the electronic map of the United States showing all the airborne aircraft. Thousands of airplanes. Then fewer. And fewer. And fewer. And finally, the map was blank. Watching the map that morning was chilling." [4] She had only minutes before been in Secretary of Transportation Mineta's conference room where the two of them had been involved in a breakfast meeting with the Belgium transportation minister. The topic was jet noise and how the European Union planned to restrict it at member-nation airports.

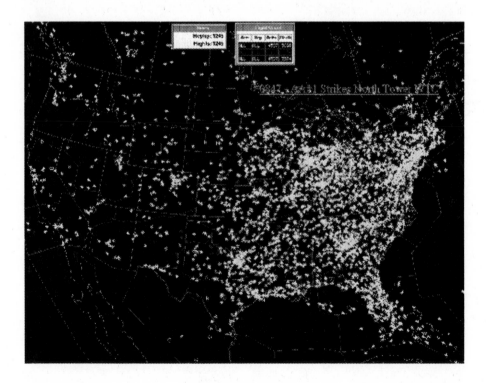

At 8:55am, a Mineta aid gently entered the room where they were conducting this high-level meeting, earning glares from his boss. Mineta was informed of the first crash. He cancelled the rest of the meeting and while Administrator Garvey flew out the door, down the street to the FAA, Mineta hurried to his office and arrived just in time to see the second plane hit. He then raced to the White House's operations center where other cabinet-level administration officials were beginning to witness what was to be a very long, and very bad stretch of events.

Earlier that morning at the Command Center, a meeting had begun the day. Linda Schuessler, facility manager, noted, "It started out as a very normal day." [5] She had arrived at the facility at her usual 5:30am and a few minutes later had strolled the floor of the building, greeting her staff as they arrived. As always, she inquired as to the latest happenings in their lives and then returned to her office to delve into the logs compiled from the last twenty-four hours of operations. It normally took nearly an hour to wade through an inch-thick report bringing her up on all the latest initiatives, facility coordination, and customer support.

She completed the report and went to the regular 8:30am staff meeting. Jack Kies, manager of tactical operations was not there, but Ben Sliney, national operations manager (NOM) for this watch, as well as several other managers from the operation attended. The NOM entered the room and explained that the Boston ARTCC had just called with the news of a possible hijacking—the same potential hijacking about which Air Traffic Director Peacock and Eastern Region Manager Frank Hatfield had already heard. Sliney, normally a participant in the meeting, excused himself and returned to the operational floor. At 8:40am, a first-line manager entered the meeting to inform them of the possible stabbing death of a flight attendant on that plane. They broke up the meeting. In the minutes it took each of them to return their meeting materials to each office, news of the first plane crash into the World Trade Center began circulating through the building. Considering the intuitive nature of this group of people, it is odd that none of them considered the two incidents—the hijacking and the crash—as being related, but according to Schuessler, something that seemed so bizarre as flying a hijacked plane full of people into a skyscraper didn't seem possible.

The Command Center functions as the traffic cop for the nation's commercial aviation industry. If a disruption occurs in one part of the nation, the Command Center routes traffic around the disruption or stops the traffic completely until the issues have been cleared up. Annually, year in and year out, the weather is without a doubt the major disrupter in the airlines' schedules, so the people at the northern Virginia facility are always maneuvering the jets around it throughout the nation. If the weather is bad in any area of the country, it can create an operational mess nationwide that they have to help sort out. Televisions located throughout the entire building were as usual turned to the Weather Channel. Weather quality across the nation immediately tells the personnel at this facility whether they are going to have a good day or a bad day. Now the tubes all focused on the CNN broadcasts.

On the main floor of the giant building staffers monitor and are in almost constant contact with all twenty-one of the nation's en route centers. Also manned on a twenty-four hour basis are desks for representatives for two industry advocates—Air Transport Association and National Business Aircraft Association—facilitating instant access to those affected by their decisions. On the wall of the control room hang several huge projection screens many of which, by now, showed CNN broadcasting the scene live. Everybody in the room still had the idea that the north tower of the Trade Center had been hit by a small general aviation craft. Then, another plane zoomed into view. It was so close and moving very fast, but many thought it just another plane moving nearer to get a better look. It was obviously a large, commercial craft. Then it hit the building.

With no time to dwell on the trauma being experienced in Manhattan, Schuessler pulled her management team together in the middle of the operations area to begin exploring all options. Field facilities began ringing the phones at the command center with suspicions of other hijackings. She was to say later, that the command center has the luxury of having telecommunications lines to all the major controlling facilities in the U.S. and because of that they could establish the big picture early. They used this advantage and began reaching out to all controlling facilities and airlines, determining if in fact other unusual incidents were occurring in the system. Schuessler said, "We started among ourselves trying to decipher the information that was coming in…The NOM, three first-level supervisors and I were gathering information from around the country that the specialists were getting." [6]

Security of the building and its occupants had to be handled as quickly as possible. The doors to the Command Center were locked and everyone who didn't belong there was escorted out of the facility. Their immediate physical safety taken care of, the management team then began worrying about any other airplanes out of control. Schuessler recalled that they "…asked them [air-traffic control facilities] to advise the command center if they had any radar targets that started dropping off the radar scope, or any deviations from their route of flight, or any loss of communication." [7]

Deluged with affirmatives about unusual events, they had trouble managing all the data. On a large white board for the next several hours the call signs and status of every plane that wasn't accounted for or didn't react exactly according to the air traffic control rules was recorded. Personnel called airline operations centers, trying to determine any crises on each flight. Only when each plane landed or was found safe did its identification information disappear from the board. Upward to two-dozen were listed at one time, but ultimately the number was whittled to eleven highly suspicious cases. Nine of those airplanes would land safely. Two of them—AA77 and UA93—would not. As the numbers of planes that would not or could not communicate with air-traffic controllers rose, Command Center management knew that all planes had to be brought down from the sky in order to ensure the safety of the passengers as well as people on the ground.

At 9:08am, all airports with planes destined for the New York airspace were ordered to ground those planes. Eighteen minutes later at 9:26am, the command center halted all departures nationwide, regardless of the destinations. Minutes later, they made it official by publishing Advisory 031. As news of the Pentagon crash was reported, Schuessler ordered her staff to announce that all aircraft had to land as rapidly as possible. Ben Sliney said, "Let's get them down!" It took less than a minute to distribute the order to all controlling facilities. Within the hour a full nationwide ground stop was announced—moments later a "land all planes" order was sent out. Advisory 036 officially closed down all operations of the national air-traffic control system.

Schuessler, still worried about the security of the facility, called the building owner and requested additional armed security. Soon armed guards were at all entrances as well as roaming the floor. As with many of the other Air Traffic managers, she had early on realized that, a record of all conversations and actions would be a must in the post mortem of the attack. She designated a staff member as scribe for each major manager in the building, requesting that the note-taker keep a record of every decision, coordination, and order given by that manager. Documentation of all actions was to be critical in recreating the events.

Not until that afternoon did Schuessler remember that her husband had been scheduled on a 9:30am plane flight originating from Dulles airport. When the thought finally struck her, she quickly raced to call him. At midnight Tuesday she left the center and went home to see him. By 5:30am Wednesday she was back on the job. Not until around 7:30pm on Friday did she finally realize the massive human toll that the attack had taken. She had at last gone home and was watching television when a news program began relating some of the personal stories of all those who were lost in the attacks. It hit very hard.

FAA Tactical Operations manager Jack Kies had been caught away from his duty post, conducting business in another part of the country. On Tuesday he was in Nashua, New Hampshire meeting with representatives of the Canadian air-traffic control organization working out the intricacies of the North Atlantic track routes—the flight paths that all airplanes take when flying between Europe, Canada, and the United States. These can and do change each day based on the most recent location of the jet stream and have to be closely coordinated with the Canadian government. Without constant monitoring, planes might be routed through dangerous and uncomfortably rough air space. As a part of his normal job as the country's national airspace manager, Kies has to concern himself with the nationwide integrity of the operation system. He says it is a daily choreography where the Command Center plays the maestro of the orchestra of air-traffic coordination "trying to make beautiful music."

As one in the cacophony of beepers resonated across the nation that morning, Kies was paged early during the attack, prior to the first crash, and told of a possible hijacking. He was startled thinking, "We haven't had one of these in a dog's age." He, as did others, assumed that it would turn out to be a false alarm. When it didn't, he headed home toward Virginia from New Hampshire. Fortunately, he already had a rental car, because none were left at the airport by the time some of his fellow meeting attendees began looking for ways to return to their homes. The drive was very long for him and two companions. As they headed south, the congestion was reasonable, but they knew that driving near Manhattan would be like moving in molasses. They mapped a route around New York City, making the trip considerably longer. The strain made driving arduous. His beeper and cell phone kept him in constant contact with the condition of the air-traffic control situation. He was enormously thankful when he got the word that all airborne planes had been landed safely. But how on Earth to get them all back into the air again? He finally reached the Command Center at around 7:00pm on Tuesday and worked until 2:00am as he and the staff Schuessler had organized wrestled with keeping the rest of the nation's air-traffic system fully aware of the decisions and rules streaming from downtown Washington.

Part of the lessons learned from the Command Center would include the manner in which the team functioned through this unscripted event. Many who had nothing to do with coordinating the ground stop, stepped into former jobs, relieving critical mangers to handle the crisis at hand. The current quality-assurance manager at the center moved back into her former job as NOM, relieving Ben Sliney of his responsibilities so he could concentrate on his duties as one of the attack response-team members. Schuessler said it was "neat to see all the effort at the Command Center and the field offices" and how well the team meshed seamlessly during the attacks.

Another FAA organization in charge of the operation of the airways facilities realized at about the same time as the ground stop order came down that a significant amount of radar data was being routinely fed into public venues such as research facilities and universities through the Internet. Not knowing just exactly what was happening and what kind of data was being used against the U.S., an immediate order was given to shut down all public radar feeds until determination was made that none of this information was being used against the airplanes and the public.

As the Command Center moved toward the land-all-planes order, the airlines moved just as quickly. Delta's head of flight operations, Joe Turner, grounded all of that airline's planes just after the second crash into the WTC. As the news showed the crashes, airline executives scanned monitors in the company's operation control center, trying to discern if any of their planes were caught up in the nightmare.

Each airline began conferring with their control facilities, working with the FAA trying to get as many of their planes to an airline hub as possible. Where they could not reach a hub, the aircraft crews had to determine where a match existed of runway requirements to their aircraft's needs. The larger airplane types used today require specific runway lengths in order to land safely—many of them thousands of feet long. Then pilots had to be sure they could familiarize themselves with landing procedures at the designated airport. Fortunately, this all occurred in the daylight, making landing and taxiing on unfamiliar asphalt a little easier. Unconfirmed reports declared that some airplanes landed at secure military bases, the closest runway on which the plane could touch down safely. Because of the obscurity of these facilities, military jets flew up, escorting these flights to the runways—less a security measure than a navigation aid.

Controllers at the Oakland ARTCC scrambled to manage the traffic. A message created later recounted the event: "During yesterday's tragic events, I was working in area G/H providing assistance where I could. I must tell you that in my 20 years of oceanic ATC [air-traffic control] experience, that I cannot remember a time that was more chaotic than it was between the hours of 0700 to 1100 on September 11, 2001."

The writer continued, "The events that led to the basic closure of our airspace occurred during one of our busiest time periods. Unless an aircraft was in an emergency status, they were either turned away from or rerouted out of U.S. airspace." Planes that had been flying all night were turned back to their destinations or sent to Canada to ensure additional attacks would not occur. She wrote more: "Almost instantly the workload at the majority of our oceanic sectors became overwhelming. Only through the professionalism and dedication of our controllers, did we manage to work through this tragedy without incident." [8]

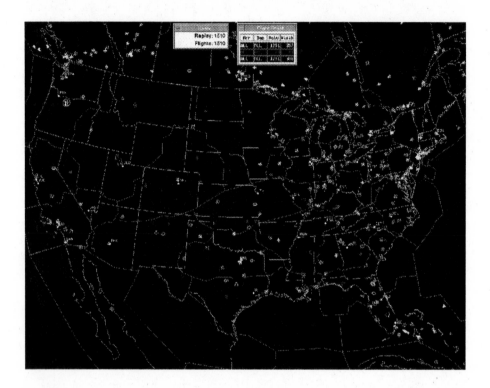

All over the nation, the controllers smoothly handed off each airplane from high altitudes, to mid, to lower until each flight was gated into a specific airport. John Carr, NATCA (controllers union) president explained, "Air traffic control is a very tightly woven net of responsibility. It is not unlike a relay race, with airplanes as batons." [9] They were guided into the pattern from the ARTCCs, to the TRACONs, over the airport, and finally one-by-one lined up on final approach to land. While the volume made it difficult to keep up, the controllers were aided by the fact that the only task was to land airplanes. If any takeoffs had been required, additional spacing would have been needed to accommodate the opposing flow of traffic. "With no commingling of departures and arrivals, and no need for en route separation of climbers and descenders, the job was simpler in many respects." Carr said, "This was not unlike a very, very heavy arrival rush for every airport in the country." [10] Only this time concern, emotion, and worry sat next to every controller. The nation was under attack.

As each plane touched the ground it was guided by ground controllers to a holding area or jetway to unload precious cargo. Within four minutes of the first order to land, about 700 planes had gotten their orders. Within another hour an additional 2,800 planes had been safely brought down. In about two and one half hours, every airplane had been safely landed. No more hijackings had occurred and no controlling mistakes had been made. It was a tremendous feat accomplished by a huge team that had never even practiced this part of the game before. One controller from Oakland ARTCC gave a figurative sigh of relief: "In retrospect I have to say that I am honestly surprised that we were able to work through this without an incident of any sort." [11] Eastern Region manager Frank Hatfield said, "What we did on September 11 was done amazingly well." He went on, "It was almost like World War II, the way the airplanes were handled."

A reporter who worked for the *Government Computer News*, often writing stories about the FAA, was aloft that day, flying from Charlotte, North Carolina to Phoenix. After the pilot guiding his aircraft announced they had been ordered to land, the writer began worrying about the number of airplanes to be landed. His thoughts were swirling: "Good Lord, can they safely guide in every flight in the air? Let me tell you, knowing only that there is some sort of national emergency going on while you are at 35,000 feet in an airliner is sobering. What if the airport control towers lose their power? What if the controllers just get overwhelmed? Of course, none of that happened and, after about 45 minutes of circling Memphis, we landed smoothly." He noticed later the stingy coverage in the press that the successful handling of the 5,000 planes received. "Nowhere in the ensuing saturation TV coverage of the terrorist events did I hear any mention of the job the FAA did in safely landing all of U.S. aviation, or just how extraordinarily difficult that seemingly simple act was." [12]

All the planes landed. Then there was the quiet. In this day and age, the background noise of a jet high overhead is the Muzak of our society, always there, annoying in a way, but also comforting. Its constancy tells us all that things are as usual. Thousands of planes criss-cross the sky, doing the business of the country on a normal day. Not today. The Eastern Region office is very near JFK airport and when the planes stopped coming, the silence was deafening. The quiet permeating the building was bad enough, but when the people stepped into the parking lot, the stillness truly hit home. The airport, home of over 300,000 operations a year, was sleeping. Even at headquarters, Planning and Procedures manager Cirillo was also considerably disquieted by the calm and called it surrealistic and odd.

By mid-morning on Tuesday, the FAA's air-traffic managers, who had been jammed into a single motel room with few phones, divided into carpools and moved to the Louis Armstrong New Orleans International Airport where they established a base of operations in the relatively secure area of an FAA facility. As they entered the airport area, they too noticed the quiet in the skies. Bill Peacock made it to the airport in one of the carpools and while setting up the continuation of his telcon learned that one of the FAA's business jets was being dispatched to spirit him back to Washington. As the plane lifted off the Louisiana tarmac a few hours later, he reflected that except for this one Lear jet and the military aircraft guarding many of the large cities, no other airplanes were in the sky, nationwide. Just for that reason, his family held their breath until the plane with him on board touched down a few hours later. One daughter had been afraid that the military might accidentally shoot him down.

He and NATCA president John Carr had spent several minutes before Peacock left New Orleans planning the execution of a stress-management program for their employees. They mobilized specialized FAA staff trained in stress management associated with traumatic events in hopes they could help many of the controllers find their way through the morass of emotions.

Peacock arrived at Washington Reagan National Airport around 5:00pm on Tuesday afternoon, one of the few airplanes to land at that location for the next month. He entered his conference room at the FAA's headquarters building a few minutes later and re-entered the never-ending telcon. With all planes in the country's airspace now on the ground and the apparent spate of hijackings terminated, that evening the focus turned to catching up on the power curve. First, Peacock contacted FAA security personnel, trying to determine the exact sequence of events that had transpired that morning. Another conference call was held with the Department of Defense, coordinating a playbook in case another wave of attacks occurred. He began working with all the controlling facilities, trying to ensure that every nuance of the attacks had been captured so future changes could be mapped and improvements made to any processes that had let the system down. Then there was Canada.

Hundreds of airplanes full of passengers, many of them Americans, were stranded in Canada. The country on the north border of the U.S. had without question come to the country's aid during the mid-morning hours of September 11. Their airports had accepted hundreds of airplanes into their airspace and onto their tarmac in order to quell any overseas involvement in the hijackings as well as lessening the air-traffic control load of many American facilities. Airports at Halifax, Nova Scotia, Gander, Newfoundland, and Vancouver, British Columbia had all taken more planes than they had room to accommodate.

Most people at FAA headquarters had only a passing idea of how many planes were stuck up there. Through yet another telcon, the air-traffic staff began determining which flight had landed where and how long each would be able to stay where it was. On the morning of September 11, Canadian controllers, airports, and even whole towns were suddenly faced with unusual situations. In Halifax and Gander, where a minimal number of flights land each day, hundreds of intercontinental flights had landed over the last several hours.

Used to controlling high altitude over-flights of international planes inbound toward the U.S. border, many of the controllers on the coasts of Canada were suddenly asked to help their southern neighbor close its air space. Considerably more very large planes would be landing at facilities not really used to this sudden increase in workload. When at 10:21am all international flights not in U.S. airspace were either diverted or turned back to their countries of origin, two hundred and thirty-nine trans-Atlantic flights were unexpectedly diverted to Canadian airports. These controllers stood the test and landed every one of them safely. Pictures of radar screens displaying the North Atlantic traffic show a groundswell of blips converging on Canadian airports in a scramble to get down.

Despite the nation's concerns for the safety and economic well being of domestic air travel and American airline companies, hundreds of international flights and thousands of people from other countries were stranded in the U.S. A huge emotional and economic ripple bubbled through the global community. In the reverse situation, thousands of Americans, flying on hundreds of flights that had been winging their way to the shores of the U.S. when the borders were closed, were now stranded in foreign countries. British Airways had twenty-one flights in the air when the attack occurred. Those more than half way to the U.S. were planted in Canada for days. Those that could, returned to their home bases to wait out the affects of the attacks. For many, it took the better part of a week to complete the flights. At some airports, jetways were grossly over-used and towns were flooded with passengers who had no sleeping accommodations. As the crowds grew, generous Canadian citizens gathered strangers into their homes and their public buildings, providing them with much-needed hospitality.

Former FAA executive Ed Kelly was returning from a leisure trip in Italy. He and his wife were on an international flight that was grounded in Canada. Worried family members searched for them by telephone for hours before finally connecting with the Kellys in Gander. Their Alitalia flight was the first to be diverted to the Gander Airport an hour before they were scheduled to land at JFK after two weeks abroad. As their plane descended from cruising altitude, passengers were shaken by the announcement that "U.S. airspace had been closed." Their plane would not be allowed to enter. No one explained what had happened until passengers using their cell phones contacted families in the U.S. Kelly knew from his decades of experience with the FAA that something earth-shattering had occurred to close the entire country, but wasn't ready for the answer. Information swirled throughout the passenger cabin. Soon the plane was fully aware that the World Trade Center towers were aflame.

After the plane landed in Gander, they sat for another three hours waiting for the Canadian officials to fashion a makeshift method for receiving all of these foreigners through customs. When the passengers disembarked, they filed past table after table manned by local clergy available for grief and shock counseling to any of the passengers. The faces of the counselors told a far grimmer story than any of the passengers knew—by now the towers had fallen, bringing the country to its knees.

As the first ones to land, the Kellys and their fellow travelers got the best accommodations the town had to offer—a piece of carpeted ballroom floor. This was to be home for the next several days. They were transported to the Gander Hotel in school buses driven by striking drivers who broke their strike in order to help the hundreds of people in dire need of support. As the Kellys entered the hotel lobby, a giant television screen introduced them to a changed world as the tape of the towers falling into giant heaps of rubble was broadcast on CNN over and over again. Kelly immediately began to worry about his brother Joe, a member of the New York City Port Authority, who worked on the seventy-fourth floor of the north tower.

At the FAA headquarters, air-traffic management coordination with the U.S. military was constant with a Department of Defense (DoD) liaison in the room and a tie-in to critical military facilities on the never-ending telcon. Early during the day of September 11, FAA, Federal Communications Commission (FCC) executives, and Department of Defense ranking officers began contemplating the invocation of a little-known relic of the Cold War. In the ultra-careful atmosphere of the possibility of instant nuclear annihilation, a kind of air-traffic control fail-safe had been planned, but never officially executed. Named Security Control of Air Traffic and Air Navigation Aids (SCATANA), it was the blueprint for grounding all airplanes flying in U.S. airspace and disabling all navigation aids that might be aiding the enemy.

Reports have the DoD issuing a military notice to airmen (NOTAM) that commanded all pilots to "follow SCATANA procedures." [13] If fully executed this would have not only forced the landing of all planes at the nearest airports and grounded those already on the ground, but it would have rendered inoperative all navigation aids in the FAA arsenal including the VHF Omnirange (VOR), VHF Omnirange/Tactical Air Navigation (VORTAC), Tactical Air Navigation (TACAN), Long Range Navigation (LORAN), and the entire non-military Global Positioning System (GPS). Combat air patrols guarding critical locations are also part of the SCATANA scenario. Most of the provisions called for in SCATANA were used on Tuesday and for subsequent days, except for turning off the navigation aids. Additional to the grounding of planes, people and airplanes wanting to fly after the ground stop were given priorities through a wartime air-traffic priority list (WATPL), giving the top priority to the President of the United States and the Prime Minister of Canada.

The one provision of SCATANA that was not executed was disabling the navigation aids. Questions surrounding the decision not to extinguish these guiding beams continued in the press for several days. Consideration was apparently given to quashing the road maps in the sky. Arguments were made for doing so because if the navigation equipment had been silenced early in the hijacking sequence, the attackers most likely would not have been able to locate their targets; but by doing so, nearly five thousand commercial jets and myriad general aviation aircraft would have been made navigationally blind. Many of the commercial jets would have been able to continue on their way via onboard global positioning satellite navigation systems, but the prospect for accidents was huge and most likely judged not worth the risk of the thousands of lives still in the air. Since turning off the entire navigation system of the National Airspace System had never been executed, even in test mode, considerable concern surfaced as to how long it would have taken the FAA's technicians to bring up and properly test each navigation system to FAA standards and put them back on line when the skies were reopened for flying. Besides, speculation exists among some quarters that the attackers had sophisticated hand-held navigation aids that could have been used until the GPS was shut down, making almost the entire action a moot point. Unless the global system had been completely quieted, the attackers would have had sufficient navigation data to fly anywhere in the country they desired.

As the managers hunched around the table in the Air Traffic conference room, stress building, they waited to see if another salvo would occur, but most of all, they all wanted to know what had happened this time. The FAA security organization, along with hundreds of others, was already trying to tie together the pieces by tracking backward through the actions of everyone in the system.

Dave Canoles and his staff began coordinating the capture of a massive number of forensic artifacts that might show how all the damage had come together—they coordinated the capture and copying of radar track data showing the exact path of each airplane. Knowing that several law-enforcement organizations would need them for recreating the attacks, air-traffic control voice tapes were acquired from every facility that had spoken with any of the hijacked planes. FAAer Tony Mello and other employees spent the balance of Tuesday afternoon, all night, and part of the next day amassing the data and coordinating with the FBI, Secret Service, DoD, the White House, and the National Transportation Safety Board, ensuring that as much evidence that was available was given to them. They had early in the day begun to ensure the preservation of the obvious data as well as flight plans of every aircraft involved, confirming all the call signs of these planes as well. Moving hard data about the country was impossible now that all planes were grounded, so they began relying on electronic means. Files containing the radar tracks were emailed to the fourth floor of the FAA headquarters where they were crudely plotted, confirming the paths of the four jets. Voice tapes were transcribed, and then the transcriptions were emailed as well.

Late on Tuesday evening, Mello's group of data gatherers needed additional equipment to handle the flow of faxes and emails. No doubt many FAA workers noticed the next day that new computers and fax machines had suddenly disappeared from normal locations throughout the building—those working through the night had done a "midnight supply" raid, liberating equipment for the investigation organization. At 2:00am they finally gave up and went home. Mello was back by 5:30am. He reported thinking that the world was coming to an end. Earlier in the day as he had passed a window and glanced out, he remembers seeing sharpshooters on numerous roofs throughout downtown Washington. He said it looked like a Third World nation with all the security visible.

Chicago visitor Tony Ferrante had gotten a couple hours of sleep and was in his office by 5:00am Wednesday, working out what had been done by his staff during the previous day and night. The most critical issue was to ensure that the radar data and voice tapes from every location involved in the attack were put under lock and key as soon as possible. Washington Reagan air-traffic manager Larry Bicknell, stranded in the Eastern Regional Office in New York City, was given the job of securing the local data to support the investigative effort. He amassed controller tapes and radar tracks for three of the four attacks. Dealing with this data up close and personal wasn't easy, but it beat doing nothing.

Part of the data-gathering process was interviewing every controller who had handled any of the four planes. Some interviews were done immediately and some were delayed because the controllers were very distraught. Also, in the back of every mind was a tension that wasn't to leave for days—was another shoe waiting to fall? Was another disaster in store for the nation? Early on September 11, the FAA had received a very credible threat to at least one of its major controlling facilities. Even though it was not publicized, confirmation of sharp shooters on many of the major buildings nationwide leaked through their host communities. Significant overhead military air support was apparent as well with fighter jets on combat air patrol above certain cities. Unseen, but appreciated was a United Nations AWACS moving to and fro parallel to the East Coast, supplied a few days after the crashes, monitoring air traffic, ensuring that no surprise air attack occurred from the ocean. Fighting ships moved to critical harbors along both coasts. Some FAA personnel, who are also National Guard and reserve military members, began packing their bags, knowing they would be called for duty on the front lines soon.

Unbeknownst to many, about midday on September 11, many FAA managers quietly slipped away from the action and were not seen until three days later. They were part of the designated group of "shadow" managers, responsible for leaving the city and getting safely to an undisclosed secure facility outside Washington, being kept in reserve in case catastrophic events in the downtown area disabled all the other managers.

Self-policing began among the FAA's air-traffic organization almost immediately. Questions arose as to why the controllers were unable to determine the hijackings sooner. As controller tapes were secured, flown to Washington, and listened to over and over again, it became apparent that only after listening to them several times, combined with an awareness of the subsequent events, could one really tell what had transpired in the cockpit of each airplane. Air-traffic manager Peacock said after listening to the tapes of UA93, "It was not easy, even when you knew what was going on to understand it from the tapes."

The recorder in AA77's black box recorded the events in the cockpit, giving the investigators a very clear picture of what went on in the cabin prior to the crash. Whatever the tapes indicate, in all cases the pilots and copilots were severely incapacitated or killed almost from the beginning of each hijacking. A fellow pilot who flies a 757 commented, "You know it was an intense life or death struggle in all of these cockpits." He explained, "They had to get the pilots out of there and kill them to pull this off." [14]

From its actions, it is also clear that despite the fact that AA77 overshot the Pentagon the first time, the large, funny-shaped building was its primary target all the time—not the Capitol or the White House as has been speculated. Targets of opportunity were not what the attackers had trained for and even as AA77 over-flew the Pentagon and was in striking distance of the Capitol, the U-turn of the flight track indicates that the Pentagon was the assigned target. On this clear and bright day, the other buildings would have been far too recognizable to have been missed if either one had been a primary target of flight AA77. Alternatively, no question exists in the minds of many who have a grasp on a larger picture through tapes and trajectories that flight UA93, which crashed in Pennsylvania, was most likely targeting one of the two prominent white buildings in downtown Washington, DC.

Dave Canoles, host of the never-ending telcon, also had the job of determining the level of service quality the FAA had provided to its customers during September 11. He began using all the controller tapes and radar track data to map any changes for the future to better manage the process. His fifteen-hour days became filled with analysis and documentation.

As part of Canoles' staff, Ferrante began reviewing the notification processes, trying to ensure that the FBI and Secret Service had been notified properly and were being given access to the tapes. He listened and looked at each tape, reassuring himself that every process and procedure had been followed correctly and began constructing a very detailed time-line of the four flights. He, along with Mello and many others on his staff, worked through several days of piecing together each move of all four aircraft. Early in the process, his hair stood on end when he realized the precision with which all four airplanes had moved toward their targets, like large birds of prey. He was to say later that, "it was almost as though it was choreographed." How had they managed such precise movements? He concluded that either they were better pilots than originally given credit for, or they had had the aid of additional onboard equipment such as radios used to communicate among all four planes. The use of hand-held global positioning system (GPS) equipment also crossed his mind. Explaining his conjecture he said, "It's not as easy as it looks to do what they did at 500 miles an hour."

Days that ordinarily began at 5:30am and went to 7:30 pm now became even longer, sometimes lasting until midnight. And even then, calls came to the executives all through the night—many of them not only had cell phones and beepers, they also had special secure satellite telephones in their homes, creating a constant umbilical cord to their work. Many of them, including Canoles' team, worked from early morning to late at night, seven days a week for the next four weeks, laboring to draw a picture of what happened and then determining what changes to make in the system to never allow this to happen again. From 6:00am until 9:00pm each day, as the entire staff endeavored to draw all the information from the system of computers and tapes, they created a little "home" for themselves in the middle of the fourth floor of the building—with refrigerators, tables, faxes, and shredders. They lived on caffeine, adrenaline, and sugar. Massive amounts of data was sifted and read, as they tried to make sense of each fact and pass the information up the chain of command to the FBI and the FAA's administrator, who was scheduled to testify before Congress within days.

Sundays were break day—no one had to arrive at work until 7:00am. As this pace continued for weeks, nonstop, Ferrante queried the group one day: "When was the last time anyone ate vegetables?" Diets consisted almost exclusively of pizza and doughnuts. One wag asked if coffee beans were considered a vegetable. At one time or another, everyone took a few extra hours off from the killing pace to manage a part of their personal lives—all except two people. Doug Gould and Dan Diggins, radar experts, were on call constantly. Working to make the original crude radar pictures more sophisticated, they spent hours and days interpreting the radar tracks of each airplane, piecing together an intricate time line that showed the actions of the giant airplanes from takeoff to crash. The hours flew by as the intensity of the work shut out their concept of time. These people only saw sunlight, fleetingly, through office windows. They came before dawn and left long after dark, becoming friends with all the people working the night shift for security and cleaning. The halls echoed eerily each night as the building emptied, leaving only pockets of workers laboring to re-establish the system and reconstruct the horrible actions of September 11.

During the first week after the attack, Canoles drove by the Pentagon, trying to get a grip on the tragedy. His horror grew as he saw the giant, smoking hole in the wall of the seat of the military command for the free world. He was moved nearly to tears. Mello had seen it a few days earlier when at 1:00am Thursday as he drove home, he turned toward the broken icon, trying to see the extent of the damage. It was still burning—Klieg lights, emergency equipment, and personnel surrounding it. Crashed concrete scattered about on the ground and smoke gently moving upward into the sky provided no answers to all his questions as he stared at the gaping wound.

The morning of September 12 dawned. Not a single non-military plane flew without long-deliberated permission from the FAA. People thought it spooky. Most were not used to the quiet and craned their necks toward the sky, looking for an errant contrail or the glint of sun on metal at ultra-high altitudes. There were none. Washington ARTCC manager Ramirez had been at the facility until 10:00pm the evening before and despite the fact that there were no airplanes to guide on this day, had shown up on Wednesday morning at 4:00am. This was to be his pattern for the next several days—running on adrenaline and very little sleep, as did most of the other FAA managers. The controllers were there and ready to work, but few airplanes moved that day. Of most critical concern to managers and controllers nationwide were the lifeguard flights—those responsible for moving organs for transplant and injured people to hospitals. Ways had to be found to put these aircraft in the air so that no additional lives were lost, compounding the terrorists' toll on the nation. Even on the eleventh, emergency flights had been necessary. FAA employee Steve King told of a call he received on Tuesday, recounting his decision that may have saved a life. "I received a call from a foreman of a coal mine in the Eastern Kentucky mountains, needing an air ambulance to take a man from Hazard, Kentucky to the University of Kentucky Hospital." An accident had severed one of the man's legs and he was in dire need of immediate help. "I called the Indianapolis Center and Lexington Approach Control to coordinate permission to fly. With all the horrible occurrences of the day, we welcomed an opportunity to save a life." Confusion forced King to cut to the heart of the issue and he told the foreman, "You tell me where you want the helicopter to land." When told the Hazard hospital, King then said, "You tell your people the FAA says the helicopter is landing at the hospital." The patient made it to the hospital and his leg was saved. [15]

As full shifts of controllers reported to the Washington ARTCC, each day after each shift change the doors were locked as a security measure, so going out for food while each shift worked was denied. The facility manager, deputy manager, and the NATCA union representative ordered mountains of food delivered during each shift, paying for it from their own pockets. During one mid shift (11pm to 7am) twenty dozen doughnuts were brought in. Everyone was not as much hungry as they were dispelling the nervous, pent up energy.

The FAA has approximately 18,000 controllers, each probably just as different from the next as night and day, but certain characteristics make them alike in the long run. Each seems to thrive on order and enjoys moving the airplanes in a systematic fashion across the sky, doing so in an almost ho-hum fashion. This is deceptive, for as Eastern Region manager Hatfield said they are almost all "alpha" creatures. The laconic attitude of controllers is as famous as the low-keyed, Southern-drawl persona used by airline pilots—voices pitched low in order to sooth those listening. But the most marked characteristic, not just in the controllers but FAA-wide, is the depth of caring and dedication that everyone feels toward his job and the agency in general. Most if not all of the Air Traffic managers who were leading the agency through this attack began their careers as controllers, working planes on the boards just like the people they manage. Personnel at controlling sites, air-traffic controllers and operations managers, work twenty-four hours a day—different personnel in three different shifts of eight hours each. Despite the fact that they really didn't have to be there, the overwhelming majority was present at every shift after September 11.

For both controllers and mangers, nerves were on high alert. Excitement spiked on Wednesday when a general aviation pilot based in Annapolis, Maryland took off in his small plane from the Midwest, apparently headed home. No one except military aircraft had general clearance to fly in U.S. airspace that day. Hackles were raised when suddenly a small blip showed up on radars in the midsection of the country. The plane didn't respond to air-traffic queries demanding that it land. It kept flying—directly toward Washington, D.C.—leaving the controllers watching the scopes thinking that maybe someone was trying to complete unfinished business from the day before. The never-ending telcon discussed the situation and finally Frank Hatfield from Eastern Region, who had jurisdiction over the invaded airspace, requested the plane be intercepted. A call was made to the Department of Defense, fighters were scrambled, and the plane was forced to land in Hagerstown, Maryland. The pilot claimed ignorance. Another unconfirmed report suggested that the military planes flying combat air patrol over and near Reagan National Airport had their own worries. More than once on Tuesday and Wednesday, intercepted radio communications indicated that military aircraft had armed their weapons in response to intrusions into the no-fly zone around the airport.

Dave Lubore, member of the flight crew on the commercial jet that had landed in Richmond, Virginia, and his pilot were still with their airplane. They had remained at the airport for hours on Tuesday, watching and waiting. They saw that many of the stranded passengers were distraught as they watched the monitors in each gate area. Lubore tried calling his family on his cell phone, finally finding his mother-in-law, requesting she pick up his son at school. He and his wife weren't able to speak for hours. He received her increasingly anxious messages left for him on his overwhelmed cell-phone answering system three weeks later. Her voice became more frantic with each message as she wondered if he was safe.

As the crew discussed what needed to be done, Lubore and the pilot decided that after everyone had contacted their families, their next responsibility was to ensure that the airplane was safe and secure. They locked up the giant vessel and headed for a hotel. The cabin crew, feeling less of a mandate for the responsibility of the equipment and the subsequent schedule, petitioned the captain to be allowed the leave Richmond and go home. It was denied. Despite the further protestations of the cabin crew, Lubore and the captain felt that everyone should stay with the equipment until the company no longer needed them. This would ensure a full crew contingent if the airplane was ordered to move. For the next several days as they stayed at the hotel, the hotel staff went out of their way to help them be comfortable, washing and drying their clothes whenever necessary.

While the crew waited, the FAA leveraged stringent new security measures into place at airports and with all air carriers. Autos moving or parked near all airport terminals were placed under heightened scrutiny and an almost zero-tolerance policy for unattended vehicles was implemented. Despite the inconvenience, curbside check-in was abandoned at all airports, as well. Access to airline gates was restricted to the flying public only, with security checkpoints beefed up to ensure no one without a ticket had access. All sharp objects were banned in carryon luggage. While each of these regulations supported the security effort, the most jarring innovation of all was the National Guard soldiers pressed into service at each airport. Many travelers were shocked at their presence, but more so by their open display of weaponry such as M-16s and other heavy artillery. This was to continue while long-term security initiatives and strict new ordinances were being put into place.

Tony Ferrante, manager of FAA investigations, worked on Wednesday responding to FBI requests for data. They had asked for radar data and controller voice tapes the day before, but now they were asking for data messages from ARINC, a private company paid by the U.S. to send messages to planes flying over the oceans and ACARS messages, a ground-to-cockpit messaging system. No one was quite sure what they were looking for, but all the data had to be gathered, indexed, and handed over as soon as possible.

All the planes in the air on Tuesday had been returned to ground safely, but now that the dust had settled, a few stories were surfacing that told Ferrante and his team that some procedures needed to be changed and tightened. The air-traffic controllers at the ARTCC in Anchorage had had a misunderstanding with a Korean Airlines jumbo jet crew the day before. The Korean personnel had queried the controller about what was happening on the East Coast based on a message received from the company on the plane's cockpit messaging system. Through a tangle of language, the crew thought they had been requested to squawk 7500, the international signal for a hijacking in progress. Thinking it was real, the controller re-routed the plane to a Canadian airport, Whitehorse, Yukon

Territory. A single Royal Canadian Mounted Policeman was on duty there. After the plane landed, the Mountie demanded that each passenger leave the plane on his command, one at the time. Gun pulled and pointed, after several tense minutes of passengers' dismounting, the policeman then turned his attention to the crew. He ordered each member of the cockpit crew to come down the steps from the plane singly after they had stripped to the waist, ensuring that they had no weapons hidden in their clothes. After the law officer determined that no hijackers were on board, the plane, passengers, and crew became the guests of Canada. A couple of days later, when planes were allowed to fly again, it was buttoned up and sent on its way. During the subsequent investigation, the three countries involved finally determined it had all been a misunderstanding, but not until some very tense moments had passed.

A major question lingering in everyone's minds was whether there had been other intended targets on which the final moves toward hijackings had never been executed. According to FAA sources, a plane that landed in Cleveland, in retrospect, could have been a fifth target for hijacking. FAA officials have no hard evidence, but have enough circumstantial evidence to convince many that at least one other plane had been singled out for attack that day. As the ground stop was announced and the airplanes rapidly descended from the sky, this particular airplane landed unexpectedly at the Cleveland airport. It had been destined for Chicago, home of the Sears Tower. Four men of Middle Eastern background deplaned and departed the airport before local officials could detain them for questioning. Another jet, an Air Canada flight scheduled to land at JFK, was caught in the ground stop. It was similar in size to the other four hijacked planes and on it was discovered weapons similar to those used on the successfully hijacked planes. FAA officials are convinced that without the rapid air-traffic control response to the brutal hijackings, additional chapters of the tragedy would have unfolded. Newspapers would later report that videotapes captured from terrorists in another country showed what could only be interpreted as potential targets. Along with the World Trade Towers, the tape showed the Statue of Liberty, Chicago's Sears Tower, the Golden Gate Bridge, and the Brooklyn Bridge.

Jumbo jets of all kinds had been landed willy-nilly at the nearest airport when the system had been closed and now were out of position for scheduled flights. Planes that had landed at St. Louis were actually needed in Florida and planes that had landed in Phoenix were needed in Chicago. The start of each flying day is reliant on a certain number of airplanes being in the right place at the right time. Many stranded planes had to be allowed to move to their final destinations so when service was re-started, all flights could be accomplished smoothly, but security rules had to be fashioned and implemented before anything could be moved. Stranded passengers had to be re-arranged, including those left in international locations. Airports had to be secured and personnel trained in response to the new security rules. On and on the list went, trying to repair the disarray of thousands of people, planes, and airports.

As the upgraded security regulations were executed at each airport during the next couple of days, a very limited number of planes were permitted to move from the airport at which they had been forced to land to their destination points. Ticketed passengers were allowed to re-board and finish their interrupted flights. In other cases empty airplanes were moved so when the system was allowed to open again, they would be in an optimum location to serve the public. Once each of these planes landed, it was uncertain as to when they would fly again, because no one could predict when the final version of the new rules would be in place, or when the airports would be able to comply with their requirements. Secretary Mineta was strictly against rushing in the face of the new security requirements. He warned everyone to be patient. "Safety is always of paramount importance, and in these extraordinary times we intend to be vigilant." [16] Not bowing to pressure already mounting to reopen the airports to all traffic, he continued, "I know all Americans want us to move as quickly and prudently as possible to return our transportation system to normal and we will as soon as we can do so safely." [17]

Most of today's flying public is too young to remember, but September 2001 was not the first time very stringent security methods had been implemented at airports. In the 1970s, when bandits and dissidents used airplanes and airlines as vehicles to express aversion to policy issues of various countries, hijackings became commonplace. So commonplace that President Nixon demanded something be done. "The result was an FAA Emergency Order issued on December 5, 1972. Airlines were given one month to implement electronic search of all passengers and inspection of their carry-on baggage. Operators of air carrier terminals were required to station armed guards at the boarding checkpoints within 60 days." [18] It was the first intrusion of security onto the passengers. Unprecedented, the flying public absorbed this new nuisance into its increasingly busy schedules, with some trepidation, as a tradeoff for the improved convenience of flying. This time, the public welcomed it.

On September 11, Washington Reagan National Airport had been closed sooner than most other airports because of its proximity to the downtown Washington area. It serves as aviation's literal and figurative gateway to the capital of the United States, with a new high-profile terminal—the showplace of the Potomac—and is enormously important to both the economy and perception of the health of business in the District of Columbia. As time wore on, it became increasingly apparent that re-opening this airport due to all the security concerns was going to be a more difficult job than with the other airports. Direct opposition to its ever opening came again from both the National Security Council and the Secret Service. It was a blow to supporters of the airport. This facility had been approved by none other than President Franklin Roosevelt on September 27, 1938. Upon opening on June 16, 1941, it became the pride of the capital and a model for the rest of the nation. Now, it might not ever reopen.

The FAA became the airport's advocate, working with security personnel and the Department of Defense. New flight approaches were planned and a security password routine was developed for the controllers and pilots. A new northern approach, different from the old one that wound its way down the Potomac River, was straightened so controllers could immediately determine any deviation from the route that might threaten Washington or the Pentagon. Still, security personnel responsible for the safety of both the city and the military reservation were not willing to take the risk. In support of opening the airport again, Eastern Region managers, including airport operations manager Larry Bicknell, were asked to comment on various scenarios that might allow the airport to function. One of these schemes was to allow landings only from the north and takeoffs only toward the south thereby taking the Pentagon and the other enticing Washington landmarks out of the equation of another hijacked airplane. Diagonal runway 15/33, used for short landings and takeoffs directly over the Pentagon, was of particular concern.

Bicknell had returned to his duty station as manager of the Reagan National Airport air-traffic control tower by Friday after the attack. He was one of two managers of all the personnel who worked in the tower. As the needs of the never-ending telcon became apparent, both managers were ordered to begin staying for long shifts at the tower, standing watch over the communications system in case a new crisis should require instant reactions. For the next several weeks, Bicknell and the other manager stood twelve-hour watches, constantly in touch through the telcon with all the other major controlling facilities in the country.

7

As Tuesday's events calmed, almost immediately organizations within the FAA began aggressive advocacy for returning the National Airspace System (NAS) to working order. After the ground stop was complete, much work was to be done. The entire commercial air-traffic control system had come to a halt. A giant had gone to sleep. If a plane was in the air for the next two days, it had rare dispensation from the FAA to fly and was monitored very closely, to the point of in some cases being escorted by military fighters. To be sure, the equipment of the system was never turned off; it was just no longer being used. But even this situation had previously never been allowed to happen. In fact, the entire agency fights each day, ensuring that every aspect of the system remains fully functional. Now, a process had to be created to wake the sleeping giant in a very orderly fashion—to begin using the software and hardware in a manner that did not surge and overload the equipment.

First and foremost, stringent security preparations at the airports were necessary. Coordination of thousands of people in thousands of cities was required. Air marshals would have to be added to many more flights than was normal; but the FAA didn't have them. Requirements for recruiting proper personnel fell to Jeff Klang while Pat McNall, Tony Washington, and Christian Jordan from the FAA's legal office worked seven days a week drafting documents used to make agreements between different agencies so the air marshals could be utilized properly.

The concept of armed marshals flying on threatened flights had originated in mid-1961, beginning with law officers on loan from the United States Immigration and Naturalization Service. By 1962, the FAA had graduated its first class of peace officers that was sworn in by Attorney General Robert Kennedy. They were used on special flights at the discretion of the airlines or the FBI. [1] Now it seemed as though they would be needed on a huge number of flights in order to protect the flying public.

As the post-9/11 security picture cleared, notification of new processes, restrictions, and requirements were developed. The FAA's Airspace Management organization wrote temporary flight restrictions (TFRs), sending them up the FAA management chain for coordination and agreement. Sabra Kaulia, manager of the

Airspace Management organization, was responsible for ensuring that each one of the messages was accurate, clear, and distributed properly. The TFRs covered just about any restriction for both commercial and general aviation flying, and could be as simple as directing that no one could fly within fifteen miles of the World Trade Towers, or as complex as the new northern approach to Reagan National Airport. A representative for the service organization Airline Owners and Pilots Association (AOPA) was available in the office next to Airspace Management manager Kaulia's, ready to interpret each TFR and explain its affect on the non-commercial flyers.

This temporary industry-government (AOPA/FAA) relationship served to smooth operations considerably, giving the federal rule makers a feel for the impact of each rule before they executed it. Melissa Bailey was AOPA's representative in the suite on the fourth floor of the headquarters building and despite not being a federal worker, she also experienced thirty to forty days of non-stop work, supporting data for and executing a web site used nationally and internationally that was regularly getting around two million hits a day. It was in many ways the most important and direct method of communication with the general aviation community. She and others in the organization knew that as long as the non-commercial airplanes were grounded or restricted, money and livelihoods were being lost.

The TFRs were provided to the pilots in a notice to airmen, sent through the FAA's Command Center and distributed throughout the nation. The NOTAM system in the United States is the communication method used to define for controllers and pilots (both commercial and general) the rules of the day. In a system as large as the one used to safely move air traffic over American territory, the status of equipment, airports, and rules change each day. The NOTAM system is the medium used to distribute these changes to all the pilots and controllers. If a runway in San Francisco is closed for repair, a NOTAM is published so that all incoming flights will know of the closure before they arrive in the area. As the system was employed in the hours and days after the Tuesday attack, the NOTAMs became almost book-like in volume. Included in each notice were instructions of all new security directives for the entire flying public. General aviation had extremely severe constraints at first. Commercial air traffic rules were no less severe, but they were more easily implemented because the commercial pilots were used to flying within a large set of rules. The notices read like legal documents:

"EFFECTIVE IMMEDIATELY UNTIL FURTHER NOTICE, ALL COMMERCIAL AND PRIVATE AIRCRAFT FLYING IN PROXIMITY TO NEWLY ESTABLISHED OR CURRENTLY EXISTING RESTRICTED OR PROHIBITED AREAS WILL BE SUBJECT TO BEING FORCED DOWN BY ARMED MILITARY AIRCRAFT. THE MILITARY HAS INDICATED THAT DEADLY FORCE WILL BE USED TO PROTECT THESE AREAS FROM UNAUTHORIZED INCUR-SIONS. HOWEVER, THE U.S. MILITARY WILL USE DEADLY FORCE ONLY AS A LAST RESORT, AFTER ALL OTHER MEANS ARE EXHAUSTED."

As the NOTAMs flowed from headquarters to the Command Center for transmission, the system crashed several times, creating frustrating and dangerous delays. The equipment in use at each flight service station (the facility used by general aviation pilots to file flight plans and receive briefings), made up mostly of old technology with inadequate memory, was only capable of producing fifty-five pages at the time. The complex security data was creating documents far larger than that. The system kept crashing. Kaulia's team focused on unraveling the notices, slimming them down by any means. People spent hours rewriting the notices, splitting some of them, sending them in several parts, or in other cases, making them pertinent to each ARTCC. The airspace encompassed by each center is like a part of a large interstate highway in the sky with different rules as one passes from one piece of the interstate to another. So the Airspace Management team at headquarters could address specific rules based on the area of the interstate they patrolled. The NOTAM team struggled with many of the operational messages, finally using one word in the place of ten until at last, late into the night, the messages all fed into the equipment smoothly, without halting the entire system. Those working the system at the Command Center became the tail of the dog, sending out page after page of NOTAMs, only to have one of many law enforcement agencies change it at the last minute, necessitating the re-transmission of the changed information.

All of this was happening at the speed of light and none of these personnel, including Kaulia, had time to reflect on the events of the week. In the back of her mind she worried about a friend who worked for the New York Port Authority in the World Trade Towers. In the front of her mind, she searched for ways to keep the rules flowing to the pilots across the nation. For thirty days straight, her team's days began at 4:00am and hers ended at 11:00pm. Everything was coordinated with the Department of Transportation, which coordinated it with the homeland defense group at the White House and in turn the Department of Defense.

Initially, all waiver requests to the ground stop had been routed to the never-ending telcon in the Air Traffic conference room at FAA headquarters, but the numbers became overwhelming so the Command Center in Northern Virginia began fielding these calls. They came in twenty-four hours a day and varied from numerous requests for flight clearances for emergency operations by law enforcement agencies to personal requirements. A phone bank was set up in a large conference room in the building. Eight to ten people sat at the table answering phones for hours each day, trying to respond to each request as it came in. Based on a prioritizing process managed by the FAA, some were given waivers, but others remained grounded. The National Transportation Safety Board (NTSB), responding to its mandate to investigate all major transportation disasters, requested a waiver to be allowed to fly their teams to New York City and Pennsylvania using planes stationed at the executive aircraft hangars at Washington Reagan National. They were denied clearance. High-ranking government personnel requested permission to return to Washington. Many others, such as governors needing to meet with the President, requested flight clearances almost daily. Some even wanted to fly into Reagan National Airport, which was still closed to almost all traffic.

Even the FAA planes needed waivers to fly. Normally, a fleet of FAA planes headquartered in Oklahoma City is in the air daily, running routines called "flight checks." This is the process used by the agency to check that all National Airspace navigation aids are functioning properly. Each type of equipment—VOR, ILS, and others—is checked by an airplane from the air, ensuring that it is fully operational and providing the proper navigation data to every airplane. Not a single system had been turned off since traffic had been grounded, so it was imperative that flight checks continued. Every time a check was needed, Oklahoma City contacted the Command Center for permission to fly.

Many of the TFRs affected businesses, and waivers were required so that industries could continue functioning. First and foremost, early on Tuesday work began to return the emergency aircraft to the air in New York City. The ground stop had exempted only one set of aircraft—the firefighting planes flying in the West. Frustratingly, the medevac and law enforcement airplanes in the hardest-hit area had been pressed to the ground until ways were devised to quantify each pilot's security risk. Maintaining constant surveillance and communications with each vehicle on what would have normally been a VFR flight became a very knotty problem within the confines of the city. Personnel in Mike Cirillo's Planning and Procedures organization literally pieced together security measures on the fly. Within hours a method had been cobbled together allowing the New York craft back into the air.

Then Cirillo's group was faced with an almost equally important, but much larger problem. Aviation permeates every corner of the nation and the world today. The longer the U.S. portion of that industry was out of commission, the more critical the impact would be. Notably, an incredible number of small businesses rely on the daily movement of aircraft. Almost immediately after the ground stop was executed, the FAA became flooded with requests for planes to return to the air, creating a huge quandary—how could they do this, but with a guarantee of safety for the public? In the South, the cotton crop was at a critical juncture, needing planes to spray against crop-damaging insects. An encephalitis outbreak was threatening another region and mosquitoes had to be subjected to an aerial spray routine. Inspectors were responsible for the maintenance of oil transportation pipelines, whose days require flying hundreds of miles over pipeline rights-of-way. Lobster wholesalers in Maine were desperate to move their crop of crustaceans to market throughout the nation. Scenic tour guides, hang-glider companies—on and on went the list of desperate voices coming through the phone to the FAA managers begging to be allowed to fly their planes again. The heavy-lift helicopter companies used in the Massachusetts cranberry bogs to lift the harvest to high ground applied to go back into the air as soon as possible. The cranberry crop was in danger of spoiling in the bogs. The farmers needed help as soon as possible.

Cirillo said later that all the FAA was very aware that for each hour the planes were grounded, honest citizens were being deeply affected. It became an effort in balancing, allowing as many airplanes back into the air while looking for the needle in the haystack that might be another threat to the public safety. The agency thought it had found the next threat when reports began surfacing about some of the hijackers who had died on the four crashed planes being recognized by the crop-dusting industry. Pictures of the attackers published in newspapers confirmed to many of those companies that their industry had been tested as a means of spreading destruction. Their entire industry was grounded and under intense scrutiny. Through contact with many of the small-business owners, Cirillo was to discover a new appreciation of the depth and breadth of the aviation industry.

The Command Center in its role as the broadcast point of hundreds of the NOTAMs from headquarters was responsible for answering questions about them. Only seven people staffed the NOTAM section at the facility—an activity that required monitoring and action twenty-four hours a day, seven days a week.

Initiatives were being published constantly and the Command Center had the responsibility of clarifying thousands of words for pilots and constituent organizations all over the nation. So many words and restrictions were being issued from headquarters that as everything was documented and illuminated, a new report was created and distributed throughout the front-line organization every two hours. For weeks and weeks the Command Center actively answered puzzled pilot queries. Pilots became just as frustrated as everyone else and began to demand, "Who made up that rule?" Time and time again, the staff stopped and explained the rationale behind the rules and managed to soothe the pilots not used to working under such intense restrictions. As with all necessities, it was the mother of invention. Innovations were tried and used or tried and discarded on an hourly basis. One that worked was the Internet and Intranet. Instead of faxing all the information as usual, the staff resorted to emailing it instead.

On September 11, Air Traffic liaison Rick Hostetler, after hours of struggling, finally reached the Command Center in Northern Virginia, which was to be his home for the next thirty-six hours. Having been caught on the wrong side of the Washington Beltway, and after a couple of hours and several detours to reach the facility, he immediately began working with all the critical agencies determining which airplanes had a crucial need to return to the air. The original NOTAM grounding all airplanes had exempted the fire-fighting planes being used in the west to fight forest fires, but no such exemption existed for planes used to fly money around the country. Federal Reserve Banks have historically used civilian aviation as one of the major methods by which money is moved from one place to another, ensuring that United States dollars are distributed properly both nationally and internationally. Without the constant, worldwide movement of American money, many of the planet's most important economies would collapse within days. These flights had to be put back into the air as soon as possible.

Hostetler and a group met with the Federal Reserve Board during the days immediately after the attacks, scrutinizing their contingency plans for means to help them begin moving money again. Oddly enough, as Hostetler found out, cash is not the most critical commodity transported each day, but it is the checks that must be moved from one bank to the other as quickly as possible in order to facilitate the cash flow for millions of businesses and banks. New methods for transportation of the money and checks were chosen and executed before the nation felt the pinch. The need for security doesn't allow discussing it, but it's a safe guess that for several days, the trains and trucks of the U.S. were carrying a richer cargo than normal.

Next, Hostetler worked with representatives from the FAA's Air Traffic organization, airports, Transportation Secretary Mineta, the White House, and a myriad of others creating a priority list for plane movement. They finally hammered out a process that allowed the stranded air carriers to move their planes. After the commercial air carriers and airports had met the new security rules, they were to be allowed in the air—American air carriers first—then the freight companies such as Federal Express, finally the foreign carriers could fly into the country after they had met the new security rules. Last, charter companies would be allowed to return to the air after they too had met their new security criteria. Until all the new rules were put into place, Hostetler's main job was the coordination of moving critical government personnel around the nation as key people from many agencies were needed at scattered locations throughout the country. Hostetler was also involved in meetings with the military, trying to coordinate the constant presence of the combat air patrols over many large cities. The difficult mix of airplanes to have in the sky—commercial and military—required constant coordination and communication, ensuring that neither organization did anything of which the other wasn't completely aware.

Even before any of this was accomplished and the airports were reopened, critical aircraft movement had to be allowed. Along with the Federal Reserve Board, the U.S. Postal Service was critically affected without the use of commercial air transportation. The Federal Emergency Management Administration (FEMA) functions as the coordinator of all domestic emergencies and they had to have immediate access to airspace and clearance to begin moving emergency response teams from around the nation to the stricken areas. Search-and-rescue teams had to be flown to New York City as quickly as possible. A hurricane was forming in the Gulf of Mexico and with the ground stop still being fully enforced, none of the workers resident on the offshore oilrigs could be moved from the storm's path. Permission was granted for the rescue of the stranded oil workers, but not so for one hiker left to his own devices in the Alaskan wilderness for a few more days than planned.

Most of the wilderness hiking done in Alaska includes being dropped off by plane with one's provisions for the allotted time of the excursion. One hiker had been dropped off the week before the attack with ten days of food. As the appointed time for his pickup arrived, no one came to retrieve him. All planes were grounded. His food dwindled, yet still no one came and he hadn't a clue as to why. A law enforcement plane, not properly equipped to land in his area was at least able to drop him a note telling him it would be a couple more days before he could be retrieved, but still no explanation. Finally, with his food almost gone, the trekking company received permission to land and return the hiker to civilization. Understandably, he was angry at being stood up until he learned the reason. Overall, Alaska was allowed to return to normal flight before the rest of the nation because often no other means of transportation or communication exists there. Inhabited areas are sometimes only accessible by plane, so the FAA gave the state dispensation as soon as they could. Rules were very strict in the lower forty-eight states, though.

One poor soul who had flown his float-plane from Montana to Canada for a short vacation realized that after the attacks, he would not be allowed to fly back into the U.S. New rules in effect demanded that all planes of American registration have a transponder. No one could fly over the border without one. Days passed and he continued petitioning for a waiver. Even if available, transponders are expensive so he was stuck. His medical practice was foundering and his family was alone. Finally, he contacted the waiver phone bank at the Command Center with an idea. "What if," he asked, "I flew my plane to the Canadian side of a lake that straddles the border, landed, and floated across the border into the U.S.? Would that qualify to get me home?" The FAA waiver writers not only agreed to his scheme, but had to chuckle at the man's ingenuity.

A life flight at the Mexican border called for permission to fly a patient to Galveston, Texas, for a heart transplant. The waiver was granted. FAA employees went to bat for many of these flights, not wanting to add another life lost to the giant list already being tallied in the three crash areas. In Nashville, home of Vanderbilt University Hospital, a tiny heart was packed in ice waiting for a flight to take it to Houston. The skies were closed to all planes but military. Sherry Jensen, Nashville Air Traffic Control Tower manager, was contacted for permission to fly the heart to Texas. Knowing that a civilian airplane probably wasn't going to be allowed to fly, she and several other FAA personnel manned the phones, trying to find a way to save the day. Nashville FAA operations manager Mark Herron began calling people, never taking "No" for an answer. After dozens of phone calls, finally a Tennessee Air National Guard team was assembled. All the while, through other lines of command, the air traffic team was arranging for waivers for the military team to fly in the quiet skies. Hours later the heart was transplanted into the critically ill infant, saving the child's life.

Everyone realized that waivers would soon be needed for special events such as flying near the Super Bowl, Daytona auto race, and the Olympics. A forty-mile security zone was established around Salt Lake City days before the Olympics began. No-fly zones were also established over other events as well—all minds were trying to predict terrorist incursions and be able to stop them before they began. Heads were bent over desks from early in the morning until late at night, defining the fine line between the need for access to the skies and the security mechanisms that would allow anyone to fly again. All were eventually worked out, but restrictions were heavy.

Former President Clinton was stranded in Australia where he stayed a couple of extra days before his flight came high enough on the priority list to be cleared for return into American air space. Ambassadors from various countries sought clearances to fly out of the country and were told to sit tight until the turmoil dissipated. After weeks of managing the waiver system at the Command Center, the process was moved back to headquarters where Tom Davidson took over.

By now, the people at the FAA were bone-tired. Despite the long hours, each came to work every day, trying to combat the yearning to stay home. Almost to a person they decided that, "We are not going to live in fear." As with many in the nation, their work became a way to strike back at the terrorists and do good in the face of all the horror and trauma that had been visited upon their communities. The staff was so dedicated that manager after manager voiced amazement at the intensity in the halls of the FAA facilities. Manager Cirillo commended his staff, saying it was his honor to get to work with every member of his team. His pride grew in the hours subsequent to the attack when he saw the line of people streaming into his office suite, volunteering for any task they could find.

Shortly after the attack, former FAAer and current Volpe executive Karen Cronin called the Federal Emergency Management Administration (FEMA) headquarters emergency center, volunteering to help. Quickly conscripted, Cronin drove from Boston to Washington, DC on Thursday, September 13. Learning that the FEMA center was grossly understaffed, she arranged for as many FAA employees as FEMA needed to be loaned to the emergency center. Many were logistics specialists, trained in managing the flow of equipment, supplies, and personnel into needed locales. Before leaving Boston, Cronin sent a list of names to the FAA of all the personnel needed. When she arrived at the FEMA headquarters after driving for eight hours, the FAA recruits began pouring in, relieving the already overworked FEMA personnel.

FEMA had launched their Federal Response Plan, through which is established the duties of every agency during a national crisis. In response, for days, Cronin and the FAA team manned the FEMA center in twelve-hour shifts arranging for the transportation of personnel and equipment into the ground zero areas. Rescue teams from across the nation volunteered and boarded special flights waivered through the FAA system to fly into the stricken areas. They were brought into the New York City airspace through the coordination of the FAA

Command Center. Worried about possible poisons coming from the fires at the World Trade Center, numerous air-sampling flights were made directly over the site, also in coordination with the FAA and FEMA. News helicopters and airplanes also sought permission to fly and get near the site.

Other FAA employees, who could find nothing to do directly supporting the lifting of the ground stop, soothed theirs and by coincidence the nation's nerves by showing the nation's colors. In Albuquerque, FAAers Mike Riley and Rob Morris hung a huge American flag on the south face of the air-traffic control tower. It is the first thing anyone landing at the Albuquerque airport saw—big, bold, and beautiful—a greeting from proud people.

In Atlanta, FAA employee Susan Ball and many others in the region felt the blow caused by the terrorist attacks. Wanting to unite them with the rest of the nation, Ball decided a flag would be appropriate. After she received Atlanta air-traffic control tower manager Gary Jackson's blessing, she set about finding a flag to drape on the tower. Ball turned to the owner of Peach Tree Peddlers, a local business that displayed sizeable flags. After asking the owner about buying an oversized flags, she was loaned one of the giant banners. With dimensions of 30x60 feet, it was very heavy, stored in a barrel to keep it clean between uses.

On the Monday after the attacks, Ball, her husband Mike, and several other FAA members took a day off from work and wrestled the mammoth flag up the stairs of the control tower by hand, trucking the storage barrel one step at the time. As they struggled upward, Sue worried about how to deploy the flag over the side of the tower with grace and respect. Husband Mike had devised a way of attaching golf balls to the back side of the flag in a manner that would allow them to tether all the corners and edges without harming the fabric, but just pushing the flag over the side seemed a little casual. Ball and her team carefully placed the flag on the ledge of the tower, readying it to be eased over the side. Finally, with the flag was in place, they gave it a gentle push and nearly 2,000 square feet gently unfurled in the breeze. As it opened to its full glory, planes stopped on the runway. Hometown company Delta Airlines called immediately, congratulating the team on their patriotism. Phones began ringing madly as people called Ball, applauding her effort and telling her what it meant to people who worked there as well as those passing through.

FAA Southern Region manager Carolyn Blum, in New Mexico on the day of the attack, was grounded there for several days afterward. She hadn't heard of the newest decoration on the air-traffic control tower in her hometown. As her plane landed and she saw the flag for the first time, it moved her to tears.

The first time Ball visited a remote FAA office in the area, she received a standing ovation for her efforts. She is quick to credit her husband and the rest of the team for actually hanging the flag, but admits that it was her idea. As a favor a local FAA technician, who is allowed to move over and through the runways freely, drove her across the airport to the perfect vantage point for taking a picture. The photo is now used on the covers of FAA documents and has been flashed all over the country as an inspiration to everyone who needed a lift.

Flags seemed to be the symbol most comforting to everyone. Pat Mairoca of Youngstown, Pennsylvania called upon a nearby military base for a flag and was rewarded with a giant banner measuring 20x40 feet. It hung on the Youngstown-Warren Regional Airport Tower, proudly dwarfing the actual tower control cab. Mairoca told the October 1, 2001 FAA newsletter *Intercom*, "Every plane that departs or arrives at Youngstown tells us that this display is a most welcome and beautiful sight." [2] School children cheered when they spotted it from a school bus on a nearby road. People at other towers followed suit, including FAA personnel in Orlando Tower who donated $1,000 to buy the enormous flag that hung on their tower.

On September 11 when the Air Force had scrambled its fighters to protect New York, Washington, D.C., and to fly on station between Pennsylvania and

Maryland, the military command structure discovered that they had no way of directly communicating with the fighter pilots. All orders from the Department of Defense hierarchy had to be relayed through the commercial air-traffic control system and if it had come, the "Shoot to kill," order would have been relayed to the military pilot by a civilian controller, because the military couldn't do it directly.

Recognizing this as a critical shortfall in the communications process, the Air Force immediately set about rectifying the problem. It could only be done effectively and efficiently by getting help from the FAA and its already-established spider-web type of communications system. Operation *Noble Eagle* was born—its mission, to add procedures, equipment, and software onto the nationwide communication system used by the FAA's air-traffic controllers so that the military could talk directly to its fighter pilots. The FAA's side of the project was put into the hands of Gregg Dvorak. He was the manager of Operational Support Program, a part of the other "half" of the FAA.

Within the FAA, the missions of several distinct groups of organizations are quite different. One of these is the air-traffic control division that consists of all the people it takes to control civilian air traffic for the United States. Another side, Airway Facilities, consists of all the personnel it takes to ensure that the systems used by the controllers are installed and functioning perfectly every day, twenty-four hours a day. Included within this organization are the technical staff, who not only plan the installation of new and complex systems, but also maintain them after each system is commissioned into the FAA's suite of equipment. It was within this section of the FAA that Dvorak served as manager.

A couple of days after the attack, Dvorak made his way back to his office at headquarters in Washington, D.C. When the assault occurred, he had been in the Boston area giving a lecture. Like millions of others in the world, his first view of the flaming World Trade Towers had been on a super-sized television screen in the lobby of a hotel. Recognizing the attacks for what they were, he sped to the nearby Boston ARTCC. Upon his arrival, he began transcribing controller tapes as an FBI agent tensely stood watching over his shoulder. He worked for several hours hammering out an exact record of what had been said between the center's controllers and the pilots of AA11 and UA175. Just as Dvorak finished, the FBI agent took his only copy of the document and disappeared. Dvorak then began monitoring and answering questions on Air Traffic's never-ending telcon and another telcon being used to determine the operational status of the National Airspace System. This continued for two more days before he could finally break away and drive from Boston to Washington. When he returned to the capital, and entered his office in the glass box office building, he found that his usual job of being responsible for the operational status of the air-traffic control system had blossomed into something more exotic. He had just become the manager that was responsible for fixing the Air Force's communication and surveillance problems.

Years of concentrating on enemies from outside our borders, federal law, and an economic imperative has supported the Department of Defense's policies of ignoring surveillance and communication matters in the interior of the country. With one notable exception in modern times in the United States (the Civil War), every enemy has come from outside, so not only was there little or no military communication capability within the U.S., the military's entire radar capabilities were focused from the extreme borders, outward. Billions of dollars were spent during the Cold War ensuring that the Russians never sneaked up on the country, but minimal funding was provided looking inward—there was no need.

Also, a legally binding civil liberties tenet has kept all federally maintained armies functioning almost exclusively outside the country's borders. Passed in 1878, the *Posse Commitatus Act* was aimed at ensuring that federal military forces were not politicized, but re-focused onto defense of the country—not policing the aftermath of the Civil War during Reconstruction. Consequent interpretation of the act included prohibition of members of the four main federal defense organizations from executing civil laws, effectively restricting significant military buildup within the U.S.

Compounding the prohibitive costs of duplicating the civilian surveillance and communication systems already in place with these two historical imperatives, it's no wonder that the Air Force was unable to effectively track the progress of or communicate with its planes on September 11.

Now all of that had changed and it became important for the military to have its own system. It also became very obvious that since the FAA was used to acquiring the types of equipment needed to correct the oversight and had the contracts in place to do so, that they should take the lead in executing the new system. The new communications requirements brought by the Air Force to the Operational Support organization were very complex, and ordinarily executing such a large program would have been very time-consuming.

Dvorak went to work, calling in experts from the FAA's Technical Center located in New Jersey. The FAA's Voice Switching and Control System (VSCS) was used as the basis for creating the new military communications system. This Harris Corporation equipment manages all high-altitude voice communications in the civilian system and with the addition of radio equipment and access to frequencies, within three weeks every ARTCC had been webbed into a short-term solution for rapid Air Force command communications with all of its fighter jets. Called "Big Voice," it basically created a hot line from a military central command to every ARTCC in the United States. Upon receiving a call from the Air Force, the ARTCC controllers were supposed to switch the hot-line call to one of the frequencies used by the newly acquired radios attached to the VSCS.

Big Voice worked very well technically, and shored up a hole in the military's defense system, but it became apparent almost immediately that this was at best going to be an interim solution. As Dvorak noted, "The Air Force likes to practice." When they did, they did so without consideration of the mission the civilian controllers have on a daily basis—controlling traffic. Air Force personnel would frequently call and request that the controller take time from controlling air traffic to switch them to the agreed-to frequencies—some of which were being used as normal civilian frequencies. The Air Force had never received the right to bump civilians off these frequencies and none of the frequencies were dedicated to this effort, so the entire scenario, while tremendously useful in an emergency, was not flexible enough to use on a non-emergency basis.

The civilian aviation structure had provided critical support of national defense at various times in the previous years. In 1940, on the eve of the country's involvement in World War II, Congress directed that $40 million dollars of the annual appropriation be used for upgrading airports determined necessary in the defense of the nation. Called the Development of Landing Areas for National Defense (DLAND), the program qualified airports for military use by a board consisting of the Secretaries of War, Navy, and Commerce. As the years have passed and the world grown more complex, coordination of this nature has become more frequent rather than less because of the intertwining nature of the aviation industry with the Department of Defense.

Sharing of the system had worked then and could work now, but Dvorak decided that there had to be a better way. He and his team determined that even as the first stop-gap solution was being implemented, they should begin planning for a final solution that completely separated the civilian controllers from any responsibilities to the Department of Defense.

The first solution had taken between three and four weeks of hundreds of FAA personnel working extraordinarily long hours to execute. It had come together faster than anyone had expected, but now that the immediate danger of having no system had been taken care of, they had to go back and create a new resolution. Dvorak commented later that he had turned the FAA's experts loose on a problem that no one had ever faced before, with an impossible timetable, knowing that they would do the right thing. They slept little, deploying equipment on the fly, making it work right the first time. Dvorak personally spent months ranging throughout the country, checking capabilities and upgrades at every location, taking him away from his family for weeks on end. He was out of harm's way on September 11, but even today his young daughter is fearful when he flies.

As he was helping define the new radar coverage required by the Air Force, several solutions were studied. As part of his research, he caught a ride on the AWACS loaned to the United States by the United Nations in the days after the attacks. They had been ordered to fly station up and down the eastern coast and he wanted to understand the plane's potential.

During the process of creating the final solution for the Air Force, months of planning and implementation resulted in radios being bought through FAA contracts and installed into every major air-traffic controlling facility in the United States, creating an independent air-to-ground communications structure for the military. Frequencies have been dedicated to the mission, negating the need to involve any civilian air-traffic controllers. The FAA purchased all the equipment and supplied as many of their talented technical personnel as needed based on a handshake agreement with the Air Force that whatever it cost, the FAA would be repaid.

In the post mortem of the attack, several additional shortfalls in the process became very obvious. As the civilian air-traffic controllers realized they were front row witnesses to the hijackings, they searched for a phone number—any number—to call and notify the military to scramble the fighter jets. Minutes were lost when they couldn't find one.

Since that Tuesday in September, two hot lines have been installed in each major controlling facility, one for the FAA to contact the Air Force (scramble out) and one for the Air Force to contact the FAA (scramble in). Calls on these lines can result in immediate launch of fighter jets to protect U.S. citizens.

Parallel to creating a solution to the Air Force's communications problems was the need for an equivalent radar surveillance system covering the interior of the country. Subject matter experts from the FAA's Technical Center were once again made available to tackle the problem. After thousands of hours of planning, contracting, and installation, teams of FAA technicians implemented a final solution for radar data transmission and have given new "eyes" to the military. By the time both programs were completed by the FAA, between 300 and 400 people had spent months, working sixteen and eighteen-hour days ensuring that each system was available as soon as possible.

At completion, the final cost was in the neighborhood of $10 million. Nothing formal had been executed between the two organizations recording the Air Force's agreement to repay the FAA. Yet, each time Dvorak would report the mounting funding requirements to acting Deputy Director Monte Belger, all Belger would say was, "Keep going." Being willing to roll the dice and gamble that the Air Force would be able to come up with the money at the end of the project was an enormous risk on Belger's part. If the money hadn't been repaid (it was) programs in the FAA would have suffered the loss.

This kind of personal investment in the mission of the FAA is a trait shared by almost everyone working for it. This attachment to duty serves to make the agency unique in ways that are not often apparent to the public, when federal employees are viewed as a mass. There is a day-to-day devotion to the organization's integrity that one can witness on a regular basis in the sacrifice of personal comfort in lieu of excessive spending. Often cheaper airline trips requiring several stops are chosen in lieu of non-stop flights—red-eye flights are chosen because they are less expensive. Travelers fly on holidays or Sundays in order for meetings to begin on Monday—all in the name of saving money and time. Technicians fret over the maintenance of equipment. Controllers strive for perfect operations. Everyone takes the FAA's role in the public trust very seriously.

Mirroring this, on September 11, the reactions of nearly thirty FAA personnel as the terrorist event was unfolding were typical of many in whose hands public safety resides. Housed in an auxiliary office in downtown Washington away from the main FAA headquarters building is a group responsible for managing much of the budget for that agency. As word filtered through the building of the unfolding tragedy, they rushed to a lobby area equipped with a television tuned to CNN. Even though none of these people were on the front line controlling air traffic, and even before it became apparent that this was a deliberate attack, they all took personally the possibility that someone in their agency had helped cause the accident. They watched and prayed, "Don't let one of us have been the cause." And they agonized over what they could have done to avoid the accident. Throughout the history of airplane accidents, everyone in the agency has personally felt the impact of each crash. Similar to the September 2001 disaster was the crash in July 1945 when a military B-25 bomber flew through a fog bank into the Empire State Building in New York City. In 2001 everyone knew that the number of dead was going to be far more devastating than the fourteen people killed that day. As the malicious intent became apparent, the FAA bystanders all reacted angrily, wanting to somehow stop the dying.

Anger and futility colored the days subsequent to the attack for everyone in the agency. FAA communications manager and *AOA Highlights* writer Jerry Lavey put words to these feelings from the vantage point of over thirty years in the agency, an answer to the prevailing question on everyone's minds. In an October 4, 2001 editorial he wrote; "What's it like at the FAA these days?" He tried putting into words the difficulty many FAA staffers were having in putting the attack into perspective. He answered, "FAA people take airplane accidents and incidents very personally. They [accidents] always prompt the questions, even if never enunciated: How could we have done better? What could we have done to prevent it?" He continued, "To most of us, it's not just a job. It's a mission, even for us pencil pushers far away from the real action." [3]

Thousands of the people serving the FAA sought ways to help guard the nation through the next hours, days, and nights. Controllers at the Washington ARTCC volunteered to stay at the center on Tuesday, even after being released to go home. Others raced to help, defining help in various ways. On Wednesday morning, September 12, when told that all non-emergency personnel—most of the FAA personnel among them—could stay at home based on an Office of Personnel Management (OPM) liberal leave policy, the *Washington Post* trumpeted the decision of tens of thousands of those who "…slipped their identification tags over their heads and went to work in downtown Washington." [4] For them, it was back to the other ground zero. As the stewards of millions of passengers each year, most of them considered this the only thing they could do to strike back at the insane acts of the day before.

Others played more direct roles in the accident sites. Eric West, a member of the FAA's Office of Investigations, was assigned to the FBI command center in New York City. Eric was struck at the tremendous devastation he saw at Ground Zero. The September 27 *AOA Highlights* gave voice to his experiences. He wrote: "An aircraft accident site always brings with it a distinct smell. The twin-towers catastrophe was no different, only on a much larger scale. Shards of building sides stood towering in a sea of total devastation. Rescue workers combed over the rubble in an effort to find anyone and anything." He searched for words and parallels and found only one—war. "As I turned around 360 degrees, there was ruin everywhere. I was thinking of all the victims and all the people, families, and businesses that must be affected by this terrible disaster. This resembled pictures I have seen of bombed out cities in Germany and Japan during World War II." [5] John Krepp, Eastern Region FAA employee, there within hours of the crash said it this way: "The destruction we witnessed first hand made the aviation accidents we investigate almost seem 'normal'." [6]

Stu Cohen and Pete Seidel, members of the FAA staff at the Eastern Region, changed into their alter-egos as U.S. Coast Guard Auxiliary members and on their off hours took turns standing watch in the New York Harbor area as part of the security blanket that was thrown over the East Coast. [7]

Eastern Region staffer Joan Brown joined the Federal Women's Program in sponsoring a drive in support of the Salvation Army, soliciting supplies for the workers at Ground Zero. They used the regional office as a collection point for dust masks, eye wash, and sweat socks. Food and financial donations were collected at the FAA headquarters in support of the Pentagon recovery. [8]

Meanwhile Gander, Canada, was overflowing with stranded airplane passengers. In just hours on September 11, the town's population had doubled as all the international planes landed and dropped their cargo onto the tarmac. Over a hundred airplanes touched down in this tiny town, and many of the passengers then spent hours trying to disembark. On one plane, participants of the Make-A-Wish Foundation were returning from a wish trip and because so many of the passengers required special transportation equipment, they were requested to stay on board their airplane for what turned out to be overnight. Some people resorted to sleeping under the wide-open spaces at the local baseball field, which turned out to be far more comfortable than the alternative—floors offered as a last resort.

Former FAAer Ed Kelly and his wife Cathy landed on Tuesday and then spent the next two days exploring the small town. Their hotel didn't have enough employees to support the vast influx of guests, so volunteers showed up from the town to scrub floors, cook, and in general watch over their unexpected guests. On Wednesday, the Kelly's asked directions to a bookstore. Without stopping to answer their question, the passerby they had questioned shooed them into his car, driving them to the bookstore, a mile and a half away. As he dropped them, he offered to return later to take them back to their hotel.

Instead, they returned to their hotel by shared taxi. As they rode, their two taxi mates told of their sleeping accommodations—the hard tile floor of a local school classroom. After hearing these stories, the Kellys felt thankful to have a carpeted ballroom floor for sleeping.

Within days of the attack, realizing that help could come from all quarters, Secretary of Transportation Mineta formed two task forces to perform quick turn-around studies analyzing measures that could be taken to strengthen airport and airline security. Chock full of luminaries, the airport security team consisted of Herb Kelleher, out-of-the-box thinker and Chairman of Southwest Airlines;

former U.S. Customs Commissioner Raymond Kelly; and president of the American Association of Airport Executives Charles M. Barclay.

The other team, led by FAA deputy associate administrator of Regulation and Certification, Peggy Gilligan, was charged with considering aircraft security improvements. This team included American Airlines Vice Chairman Robert W. Baker; former Boeing Company vice president Robert Davis; and Captain Duane Woerth, president of the Air Lines Pilots Association. Both teams were given a clean slate and reassured that any suggestion they made would be considered. Each team was urged to think unconventionally in the hopes that their solutions would move the airlines ahead of the next terrorist attack. In effect, they were looking for a new model of security in the United States.

On Thursday September 13, Secretary Mineta announced the resumption of commercial aviation traffic. Throughout Wednesday night he had been involved in meetings with a myriad of leaders from the White House, the Cabinet, the FAA, industry, and law enforcement. As the security picture resolved somewhat, he decided as each airport implemented the new security rules it could petition to open for operations. Except for Washington Reagan Airport. For all the others, he was cautious, but positive. "The re-opening of our national airspace is good news for travelers, for the airlines, and for our economy. But I must caution everyone that a system as diverse and complex as ours cannot be brought back up instantly." [9]

He was correct. Even as the controllers began moving a minimal number of planes around the skies again, stress mounted. Minute procedural errors made by pilots that would have been ignored or not even noticed only two days before brought about immediate and sharp inquiry from security-aware controllers. Halting the national air-traffic control system was a mammoth process, but nothing compared to firing it back up again. As Jane Garvey was to say later, "There is no playbook on how to restore an aviation system. There are no guidelines on how to work with national security agencies. We are working to restore aviation in a new environment." [10] It was a challenge never foreseen and therefore had no national rules. The unprecedented shutdown of the entire system within a couple of hours had never been predicted. The re-implementation of the system was equally unusual—no one had any procedure as to how to begin again.

As airports opened for business after qualifying with the new security requirements, the nation sighed with relief. But Thursday saw only 800 flights through the Washington ARTCC's airspace—a mere fraction of the normal. It would be up to 2,000 by the next day, but still far below what usually flew through the space. The rest of the nation had similar numbers of flights on September 13.

As the aviation industry and the federal government began publishing the new rules, each airport had to be re-qualified for the new security processes, forcing each to become functional at different times. Complicating the effort was the time-consuming process by which the controlling facilities had to check whether the flights with which they were communicating were cleared to fly and land at various airports. Each domestic airline was cleared as a group, but all international flights were cleared on a one-by-one basis, creating a mammoth backlog of arrivals at each coast. This meant that as each flight flew from Europe, through Canada, or from Asia, every one had to have a specific clearance relating to their call sign. Many on the verge of being handed off from Canada to U.S. controllers were disallowed based on the lack of clearance. They were turned back to their homeland or landed in Canada.

By Saturday, even though almost all airports and airlines had been cleared for business, only 9,822 flights made it into the air—compared to the normal 35,000. [11] As the traffic count mounted on Thursday and again on Friday, Operational Support manager Gregg Dvorak had technicians standing by at every major controlling location, on alert awaiting any equipment problems. Since the system had never before been completely idled and then reactivated, no one knew what a sudden influx of flight data was going to do to the computers used to run the system. Would a sudden increase of keystrokes hitting the software at once as the airplanes began to take off in massive numbers overwhelm the main computer and take it off line in one or several of the en route centers located throughout the nation? The airway facilities group monitored this throughout the first couple of days as the number of flights grew, until everyone was sure that the system was stable.

On Thursday, in Gander, airplanes were being re-boarded so passengers could be flown to their final American destinations. Ed and Cathy Kelly were relieved, thinking they would finally be allowed to go home and be reunited with their family. The plane was loaded (their checked luggage had never been unloaded) and they pushed back in preparation for takeoff. The Boeing 747 taxied all the way around the airport. The passengers were startled to see the "Welcome to Gander" sign reappearing in the windows. As they sat on the tarmac, the pilot took to the public address system, explaining to them that the U.S. airports (JFK) had been shut down again and that the company (Alitalia) had decided to return the plane and its passengers to Italy. The plane erupted. No one wanted to return to Italy.

As the passengers were on the verge of riot, the airport manager was brought on board to help calm them and explain the passengers' choices. Their luggage was going with the airplane and wouldn't be available to anyone who disembarked, he told them. He also explained that without rental cars (Gander had none) there was little anyone could do to navigate the nearly twenty-hour drive to Boston. Some passengers left the airplane in a panic only to re-board moments later when the reality of the distance to home set in. Finally calm, the jumbo jet was cleared for takeoff and the passengers arrived in Italy early Friday morning, September 14.

By then the flight data recorder for UA 93 had been found in the Pennsylvania field. Two recorders are standard equipment on all large modern commercial aircraft. The flight data recorder captures operational data on all major airplane systems, such as hydraulics. Critical in most instances of aviation crashes, it would have only been useful if a system malfunction had caused the crash. At the very least it would tell the inspectors the attitude of the plane and recount the settings of all the systems when it crashed. Most important to everyone was the recovery of the voice recorder, which if it had been allowed to continue functioning during the last minutes of the flight would have thirty minutes of voice recordings from the control deck of the airplane. But it was still missing.

FAAer Michael Shannon was sent to the Shankesville site the day after the crash, to help the FBI find the recorders. He says, "The memories of that day will remain with me forever. I remember seeing names on various scattered papers and thinking that there's a mother, father, son, daughter, husband or wife whose life has just been ripped apart by a group of thugs who deserve the worst punishment a nation and a world can deliver." [12]

Found later, the cockpit voice recorder was buried twenty-five feet below the surface of the earth in which the plane had crashed. With that recovery, the officials hoped it would divulge some of the secrets of that lonesome strip mine in Pennsylvania. Ultimately, it would yield little in the way of hard and fast evidence. Wind noise filled a lot of it as a result of the inordinately high rate of speed and low altitude at which the plane was traveling. The final struggle is recorded with significant shouting, in both Arabic and English. A woman begs for life and an American voice yells, "Let's get them!" An Arabic voice warns his accomplices, "They're coming!" [13]

By Friday, September 14, 421 of the nation's 451 airports had opened after meeting all the new security standards. Of the major airports only Boston Logan and Washington's Reagan National were still darkened. By the next day, only Reagan National Airport in Washington was still closed. Flights proceeded gingerly about the nation, but in much-diminished numbers. Many airlines had reshuffled airplanes, caught in the wrong place at the wrong time on Tuesday, so they could restart their flight sequence. San Francisco and Denver started with only about twenty percent of scheduled flights taking off. Chicago and Houston Intercontinental managed a higher fifty percent. Washington Dulles handled about twenty percent of their normal flights and Baltimore-Washington International saw off even less than that. At least the airlines were allowed to remove most of their planes from National's tarmac and fly them to other airports on September 15, 16, and 17 with the hopes that the hiatus would be short. Only outbound flights from Washington National were allowed so airlines that had been forced to land there on Tuesday could claim their aircraft—inbound flights were still considered too much of a security risk and word went out that the runways on the Potomac River were closed indefinitely.

Reagan National Airport is an icon in the nation's capital. Opened on June 16, 1941, it became a significant attraction for tourists and locals alike. Over a quarter of a million passengers moved through the airport in the first year and more than two million people visited the airport in the first six months of operation—watching a new industry in full bloom. For it to be closed after the attacks was a blow to the nation's ego. It's proximity to important national monuments and buildings posed a huge and continuing security problem to the Pentagon as well as downtown Washington, D.C. But the city was losing considerable money and the aviation industry, the local tourist organizations, and the city of Washington, D.C. lobbied for its reopening.

No one could say when and if regulations could be tightened enough to reopen this airport. Security officials were all for closing it permanently. This airport serves sixteen million passengers each year, leaving a considerable problem for the FAA and other law enforcement organizations to wrestle with if they decided on permanent closing. Under severe pressure to reopen the location, FAA spokesperson Laura Brown explained: "The security issues in Washington [National] are unique. We'll have a level of security that's appropriate for its location." [14]

Significantly, this airport has seen its share of horrific accidents, one of the most tragic in 1949 when it was the location of the deadliest accident on record at that time. A DC-4 and Lockheed P-38 crashed on final approach killing fifty-five people including two congressmen. Only six weeks later, another crash occurred with the plane winding up in the Potomac River, killing several more people. In 1982, Air Florida Flight 90 took off from there on a very wintry day, crashing seconds later on top of the Fourteenth Street Bridge, killing seventy-four people, leaving five alive, swimming for their lives in frigid, icy water. Rife with navigational intricacies, and little room for failure, it is nonetheless one of the most important airports in the country. Opening it seemed tied to making the country whole again.

Another new challenge to the air-traffic control system was the constant and sizeable presence of the military. Not only were combat air patrols relentlessly circling some large metropolitan areas, but the military command wanted to be active in the controlling process. Washington ARTCC air-traffic manager Ramirez included the military where he could, but mostly kept them at arm's length, citing safety as the reason. The military's main objective was intercepting airplanes, while as Ramirez noted, the FAA continued focusing on their main mantra—separation of airplanes. So it seemed inherently obvious to him that keeping the two organizations separated as much as possible was the thing to do.

The basic incompatibility of the two groups has been apparent since the inception of controlled airplane flight. Opportunities to combine aspects of the two have been studied and discarded for years. As early as 1963 when an interagency committee studied the feasibility of combining the FAA and Department of Defense (DoD) air-traffic control functions, the final conclusion was that operationally, the two organizations were too different for them to be controlled by the same group.

On a sporadic basis, though, the two government organizations have worked together well. During the Cuban missile crisis in 1962, hours before President Kennedy announced to the country that he was going to blockade Cuba to force them to dismantle their missiles aimed at the United States, the FAA was requested to provide a temporary air-traffic control tower at Key West, Florida. The temporary tower and the Miami ARTCC were both used to support the blockade until safety to American borders was restored and the missiles were removed from Cuba. [15]

Differences have reigned in almost every other case, though. In 1954, unique navigation tools were being used to service each community—one for the commercial airline industry and one for the military. Many times sitting at exactly the same location, the VOR and TACAN both functioned as navigation aids, one for each division of the government. A committee struggled to determine the single optimum solution to the navigation requirements of the two organizations, but because the requirements were so different, the committee gave up and was never able to sufficiently differentiate. Nearly fifty years later, the two duplicative tools still exist side-by-side. Throughout the years, as the aviation industry flourished in both the commercial and military arenas, the requirements of the two endusers has remained at odds and having to meet both objectives after September 11 created additional tension in the controlling arena.

To that end, a Joint-Chiefs-of-Staff-sanctioned group has been formed to create a Concept of Operations between the military and the FAA, as well as other organizations such as the Secret Service and the U.S. Customs Service. It was born out of the realization that on September 11, fundamental issues both large and small had to be addressed and agreed by all of them. One of the first and hardest issues turned out to be defining what to guard against.

Despite the fact that little cohabitation existed between the FAA and many of the other organizations with which they were to work on September 11, they suddenly became what amounted to best friends shortly after 9:00am that day. The FAA, Secret Service, Department of Defense, as well as numerous other groups realized that they couldn't get along without each other. FAA Planning and Procedures manager Mike Cirillo was struck that day and the days subsequent at how closely his organization began coordinating with all the other organizations, some within the FAA with whom he had never before worked closely—security, legal, and flight standards to name a few. He and the personnel in his area spent the hours and days after the attack rewriting old procedures where possible, and writing new ones when necessary to steer the industry back toward safety. He came to rely on the FAA's legal organization to help him stay out of hot water, while also looking to the security personnel to read the new procedures and find any security deficiencies. Their new relationships upgraded their coordination plan, leaving them in a position to identify anomalous events more rapidly than before the attack—creating a complex system of information sharing that had never been attempted before. In effect, the terrorists impelled the FAA personnel toward becoming an integral part in the nation's security apparatus, a place that had been theoretical until now.

The Planning and Procedures unit, as did many of the FAA's other affected groups began killingly long work hours after September 11, with days beginning well before sunrise and ending hours after sunset. On the first night, knowing that someone would have to stand watch on the never-ending telcon, Cirillo flipped a coin with his deputy, Eric Harrell. Eric lost and spent that night on watch at the FAA building. Cirillo returned at 4:30am Wednesday to relieve him. It became habit for Harrell to take the mid watch with Cirillo taking the day watch. Cirillo said with admiration and appreciation that Harrell and "a ragtag bunch of employees" stood watch together for many nights without any complaints. In key military and law enforcement facilities scattered throughout the nation, there was only one FAA person. As the demands of the never-ending telcon took over, these individuals practically never slept, because they had to remain at their posts, available to the teleconference at a moment's notice. Weeks passed before some of these people could relax and return home on a regular basis.

As each airline struggled to return its fleet to the air, the question of aviation insurance arose. From almost the beginning of passenger flights, insurance has been required for every flight. When domestic air carriers couldn't afford insurance in times of war, or when the industry simply refused to insure such juicy targets of opportunity, the federal government had a provision by which insurance would be provided. Since 1951, this had been available. Through this backing, the American commercial aviation system grew and matured through the 1950s with the availability of war risk insurance. Evolving as part of the program in the Department of Commerce, it was ultimately handed off to the FAA during its formative years. "Under the program, FAA maintained a premium standby insurance plan that would make aviation war risk insurance available at the outbreak of war." [16] Without liability insurance, no planes belonging to an airline can leave the ground. Prior to September 11, liability coverage for attacks of this sort cost the airlines approximately two cents per passenger and was handled by commercial insurance companies. In the days after the hijackings, this cost jumped to a dollar and twenty-five cents—a backbreaking cost hike for the airlines. Even at that price, the commercial market was in chaos and very reluctant to cover the airlines. Knowing that the only quick way to manage the problem was at the national level, governments in several countries anted up the insurance in order to manage the airlines back into the skies.

As a result, the U.S. and the UK both became *de facto* insurance agencies. As part of the post-September 11-attack, the two countries agreed that the first $50 million per incident in liability was the responsibility of each airline in the case of warfare and terrorism damage. Whatever might come above that, the federal governments agreed to insure, up to a total per incident of one hundred million dollars. Months of this type of coverage were going to be necessary while the private industry returned to normal.

Over the weekend after the attacks, dozens of people in the Office of Aviation Policy and Plans and the Office of Chief Counsel worked the phones. Fifty-five different policies were sold to airlines flying in United States airspace. They later dubbed their small group FAA Aviation Insurance Company. Both governments agreed to pull out of the insurance business as soon as the markets recovered enough to take up the slack, but as of the end of 2002, no end was in sight for either federal entity.

At the FAA Computer Security Incident Response Center, the normal twenty-four-hour a day, seven day a week schedule remained the same, but the work load became considerably heavier. As the FAA tightened its information security, the agency's disaster recovery plan was executed. Heightened security against hackers required significant additional staffing which was not available. As word leaked about the needs in the computer security area, qualified personnel from Information Services and the Free Flight office volunteered and began taking shifts with the regular staff. [17]

The country's two hundred thousand general aviation planes were severely impacted by the shut down. This designation includes not only pleasure planes, but also all the business jets in the United States. They were grounded. Until September 14 their pilots were allowed to do nothing more exotic than taxi their planes. One pilot, apparently misunderstanding the rules, flew into the airspace around Manassas, Virginia, the day before the ban was lifted and was quite nearly the next victim of the week as fighter jets sped to its location. Fortunately just before they arrived, the smaller plane landed without incident.

New rules were announced here too. Sabra Kaulia's group spent days working out a set of credible regulations that would allow these non-commercial planes to fly again, but the first set was very restrictive. All general aviation flights had to be under IFR with an official flight plan being lodged with the FAA. On September 14 at 4:00pm, most general aviation planes were released from the ground. Independent in spirit and much like the original mavericks who refused to be regulated in the early Twentieth Century, these operators chaffed under the yoke of additional regulation. Most of these regulations were directed at putting them under heavier controls and they were incensed to be considered as a potential threat. As Administrator Garvey said later at the 2001 Airline Operators and Pilots Association (AOPA) Expo, "Let me assure you, I know, and Secretary Mineta knows, that you are not the security risk. The individual GA [general aviation] pilot is not the culprit." [18]

Other conventions of flight changed too. Usually the airspace near an airport is managed under a set of regulations referred to as Class B rules. These define proper actions of pilots as they fly in certain parts of the airspace. At low altitudes, restrictions range outward for only a few miles. The higher the altitude, the further out each set of limits apply until a sort of an upside-down wedding cake has been created. On September 11, new enhanced Class B rules were created, allowing no general aviation planes to fly within twenty-five miles of either New York City or Washington, DC. After September 11, the restrictions had changed in shape as well, from a wedding cake to a cylinder. Not until December 19 were they relaxed and returned to the original Class B rules at most of twenty-seven affected airports. Even after restrictions were eased, critical, but less stringent modified rules were still in effect at New York City, Boston, and Washington, D.C. The New York City no-fly zone was reduced to a circle with a two-mile radius, with Ground Zero being the center. Boston had a three-mile radius, and the Washington no-fly zone was reduced from an eighteen-mile radius to one of fifteen miles, centered on the Washington Monument. [19]

As the danger waned and the government came to the conclusion that another wave of terrorism wasn't imminent, restrictions were repealed from every airport that served the general aviation community except for three that had the misfortune of being located in the shadow of Washington. College Park (Maryland) Airport, Potomac Airfield, and Washington Executive Hyde Field were all still in the no-fly zone and airplane owners with planes in these locations were grounded indefinitely or at least until a new and definitive set of security rules could be worked out. This was particularly hard on the College Park Airport. The oldest airport in the United States, it had proudly carried the aviation banner in support of the country for decades—now it was shut down for an indefinite time.

The executive branch of government was deeply immersed in the business of planning a war, but on September 14, President Bush took time out and led a national mourning service at the National Cathedral in Washington, D.C. He said, in a sentence that the members of the FAA would take to heart during the next several weeks as they struggled through never-ending days: "Adversity introduces us to ourselves." He continued to reassure his government and his country saying: "This conflict was begun on the timing and terms of others." He paused and then added, "It will end in a way, and at an hour, of our choosing." [20]

By Saturday, Ed and Cathy Kelly, still stuck in Italy, were told to re-board their airplane, only to have a six-hour wait on the tarmac at the Rome airport before they were blessedly airborne. They missed their connecting flight at JFK and finally bowing to the inevitable, booked a train ticket from New York City to Washington, D.C. As they traversed the highways and parkways from the airport to Penn Station in downtown Manhattan, they went through military-like checkpoints and saw a city under siege. Police barricades and police personnel guarded every corner all the way across town, from east to west. Having been sheltered to a certain extent from the trauma while in Europe, the reality of the experience near Ground Zero came as a shock.

FAA Administrator Jane Garvey had been waiting for days to testify before Congress, waiting to tell our leaders and the nation her story. As she completed her testimony on September 21, 2001, Garvey paid a compliment to the employees of the FAA who had struggled to bring the sleeping giant to its feet by saying: "The President said last week 'Adversity introduces us to ourselves. Our fellow

Americans are generous and kind, resourceful and brave.' I would like to include the men and women of the FAA and DOT [Department of Transportation] in that company." [21]

Later that evening, as the Capitol was readying for the President's visit, giant city buses were staged in the area and the streets were closed. Although no one at the FAA building just down the street had time to notice, the entire world had changed. Instead of carrying city passengers, the buses were parked across each access street, creating massive metal barricades so no one could approach the building. The wagons were circled and the leaders protected. President Bush's final declaration of the evening served notice on the attackers and boosted the audience's spirits. He said: "I will not forget this wound to our country and those who inflicted it. I will not yield; I will not rest; I will not relent in waging this struggle for freedom and security for the American people." [22]

8

Losses to the airlines were around $300 million a day. The normal 1.9 million passengers, 40 thousand tons of cargo, and 60 thousand general aviation flights were significantly diminished and by Day 2, the pain was beginning to show on much of the industry. As the days after the event gingerly moved past, the FAA management worked feverishly to support the faltering aviation companies. Crew time in the air, late take offs and landings, and missed connections were almost as frustrating as the lack of passengers. The safety issue became paramount in everyone's mind on September 11, while the economic support to the industry became a secondary notion. As a result, by September 12, Midway Airlines, which had already filed for reorganization under bankruptcy laws, called it quits and permanently went out of business. Others airline companies were teetering on the brink. This was a stunning blow to an industry that had spent nearly one hundred years as king.

Costs of creating and operating the massive FAA hardware network may have played a part in the outcome of the September 11 attacks. The mystery as to why flight AA77 had been so successful in attacking the Pentagon was at least partially answered when its probable track was retraced through the hills of West Virginia. There are twenty-one en route air-traffic control centers throughout the United States. These are mammoth buildings that house controllers responsible for high-altitude air space management, controlling air traffic twenty-four hours a day, seven days a week. Each center controls an established section of airspace and each of these spaces is carved into sectors small enough through which a single person can direct all air traffic. These controllers' scopes are supplied with information based on radar data of two different types. As officials scratched their heads over the loss of contact with AA77 for nearly thirty minutes on the morning of September 11, they closely scrutinized the radar coverage in the area where it was hijacked and its path as it returned to Washington.

For years, budget pressure on the FAA has necessitated choices concerning what equipment is upgraded and what is allowed to fade because no funding exists for long-term maintenance. The radars termed primary were part of the systems allowed to disappear gradually because of budget pressures. Originally, the nation was blanketed with primary radars—technology that allows a beam to "see" an airplane before the invention of transponders. These kinds of radars can provide a blip on the screen showing controllers the location of an aircraft, without the specific flight information on planes equipped with transponders even if the transponder is not transmitting. In 1959, secondary radars began to be installed in what was considered an upgrade to the air-traffic control system. The new systems tracked all individual aircraft based on the use of a transponder. Because secondary radar is technologically more user-friendly for controllers and because having duplicate radar coverage throughout the nation is very expensive, significant areas in the country are not covered by both types of surveillance. Besides, it probably never occurred to most people that an airplane fitted with a transponder would not want to be seen. Until September 11, that scenario was too unlikely to even worry about.

Just as AA77 was hijacked and its course reversed, the jet entered an area with only transponder coverage. When the hijackers turned off the transponders in this area with no primary radar coverage, the system in effect went blind, causing the plane to be able to fly back toward Washington undetected.

Economic reality was the copilot of all safety and security decisions made over several days after Tuesday. Mindful that they were tinkering with an industry responsible for 100 million jobs and 1.5 billion passengers worldwide, another kind of minuet ensued between the airlines and the federal regulators. Rule after rule was proposed, many of them creating a new economic burden on the companies. Airline executives booed at least one of them down when on Wednesday, as DOT Secretary Mineta conferenced with the airline CEOs, he announced a rule requiring a wand check of all passengers who moved past the security gate. Reported in the *Washington Post*, "The airline chiefs were stunned by the wand rule. Such changes could drive people away by the millions." As the hue and cry ensued, DOT gave ground. "Spokesman Chet Lunner agreed, 'It was a balancing act. We had to weigh the security issues while trying to restore some sort of normalcy to the system and keeping an important part of our economy moving at the same time'." [1]

FAA Tactical Operations manager Jack Kies took the problems personally as he worked through a month's worth of eighteen hour days. Based on his position as manager of the operational side of the national airspace, the buck stopped firmly on his desk: he was responsible for putting planes into the air. He said later that his only objective became helping to get as many airplanes into the system as safely possible. Safety as always was foremost in everyone's mind. Kies said of that time, "Safety concerns were unspoken, but always on the table."

By the weekend, despite the fact that airports were open and planes were flying, thousands of patrons stayed away. An action that had been as casual as riding a taxi only days before, had suddenly become too scary to contemplate. Much had to be done in order to convince the flying public that it was safe to embark on airplanes again, and the duty fell to the federal government. This problem had been met in the past when commercial air travel first became available in the United States.

Flying is not a natural state for humans and for most the trust required to do so is tenuous at best. Realizing that without regulation the industry would never flourish, the 1938 law that created the FAA predecessor was chartered in part to "…build public confidence in aviation as a safe, reliable form of transportation." [2] All confidence had been shattered by the terrorists' attacks. As the CEO of Delta put it, "It's an incredible new era. Things will never be the same." [3] So the FAA was once again faced with convincing the public that flying was safe. Despite several well-publicized commercial airplane trips by the President's entire cabinet in the weeks following the attacks, patrons were skeptical. But, as time passed, things began to improve to the point that in the long run, the problem effectively solved itself. The country's lifestyle is inextricably bound to aviation and therefore will never be complete without it. In the foreword of an FAA history book *Bonfires to Beacons*, Peter R. Clapper discusses the meaning of the genesis of the airplane to the human race and why it or its successor will always be important. "The airplane is a liberating force—a force that released him from his earthly tether and helped ease the demands of time and distance. Thanks to his machine, mountains, oceans, and vast stretches of desert, which man had previously traversed with time-consuming effort and often at his peril, today are daily conquered with speed, ease, and safety." [4] This liberation will always be in demand and will probably intensify over time. People will fly again, no doubt with considerably more trepidation, but they will fly again.

Pilot Dave Lubore flew again the very next week from Dulles. He noticed an overwhelming tenseness in every passenger and members of the cabin crew—the front line of any hijacking. All were extremely anxious. Weeks would pass before this atmosphere relaxed. Then suddenly about a month after the assaults, he recounts seeing a change happen almost overnight. He speculates that either people had enough time to put the fear of the tragedy behind them, or more likely, a new mindset had taken control. He said the difference was that they all seemed to have been given permission to fight for their lives if the same events ever played out again and they were comfortable with the thought. He theorized that if you take away the concept of security while flying, that people are more than willing to defend themselves. People suddenly seemed to understand the new rules and were willing to use them. Lubore, in the wake of missing or conflicting guidelines from airlines or the government, began taking intensive self-defense lessons and feels as though he will be able to contribute significantly to the safety of his airplanes in the future. As far as the support he received from the FAA's air-traffic control system, "They did a phenomenal job that day."

Sabra Kaulia, FAA Airspace Management manager, flew for the first time about two weeks after the September 11 disaster. She recounted how passengers were so threatened that they were all acting "weird." "The security was intense," she said, "It was strange seeing camouflage uniforms inside the airport." But the military presence and the high-profile weapons comforted her.

On Sunday, September 16, Frank Hatfield, Air Traffic manager from the Eastern Region was summoned to FAA headquarters in Washington. His experience of being in the eye of the hurricane during the attacks on the nation had made him a prime candidate for helping create a primer of how to successfully shut down the air-traffic control system if the need ever arose again. Offered a ride in one of the FAA's fleet of jets, he declined, wanting some peace, and drove the four-hour trip from Long Island to Washington. He had been getting by on only a couple of hours of sleep each night, using the rest to stand watch at the regional office on the never-ending telcon.

Hatfield joined a team of experts from the agency, including Jack Kies, Tactical Operations manager, who struggled with codifying the experience of landing all planes if another national emergency occurred. They met, discussing everything that had happened and the genesis of each action that had been taken. As the team explored the national response to each new danger, they realized that most of the instinctual reaction by managers and controllers across the nation had occurred based on experience and intuition. Kies argued that it hadn't been scripted and as the team struggled, they were coming to the realization that maybe it shouldn't be. Finally, they concluded that if a process was built from the week's experiences, people would be prone to "going by the book" as opposed to doing what instinct was telling them was right and that the "book" couldn't possibly be any better than actions taken on September 11. Kies and Hatfield left Washington a few days later, satisfied with the knowledge that nothing had been written down and if similar events ever recurred, the managers, controllers, and technicians would all do the right thing again and instinctively guide the planes down safely.

Kies said that it was best to "let the operators operate." He noted that the Command Center had been created on the basis of consolidating the air-traffic response to any situation that would disrupt the normal flow of things. On September 11, 2001, the original vision of this facility had been borne out. He said, "We were properly prepared to deal with the activities. We were perfectly positioned to react in a collaborative manner and it worked." In the 2002 annual report of the National Institute for Urban Search and Rescue (NIUSR), executives validated a similar approach to all disasters, noting that trying to take control of a catastrophic event from top down would most likely exacerbate the situation. They suggested that all command and informational boundaries be dropped during the front end of the crisis. "Throwing up barriers around the perimeter and erecting firewalls [literal and figurative] may block out essential information and resources. In the first hours, an effective emergency response is the coordinated dissolution of boundaries." [5] Whether by instinct, happenstance, or planning, the people manning the aviation control system did just that. The results have validated the method.

Two weeks after the attacks, New York ARTCC manager Mike McCormick was ordered to take a day off by two of his mangers. Instead of sleeping in or doing household chores, he took his wife and son back to New York City, the place they had only two weeks before gone for his birthday celebration. They saw a show, ate dinner, but before that, they journeyed to see the mountains of smoking rubble where the towers had once stood. He said the reason they returned was "to support the City and make sure the terrorists didn't win." They intentionally returned to the place where they had laughed while looking up into the sky, becoming dizzy when viewing the impossibly giant towers that made up the World Trade Center. McCormick wanted his eight-year-old boy to understand what had happened and not forget.

9

The final count of FAA-related deaths included one husband, one wife, and an assortment of brothers, nieces, and on and on until at least twenty-three employees had lost someone or several some ones. Former FAAer and current FAA support contractor Dan Hamilton lost four family members. Eastern Region's Bob Macchia lost a nephew, (Johnny Napolitano) a member of Rescue Company #2 of the New York City Fire Department. According to Macchia, the unit was last seen as they climbed the North Tower trying to reach victims on the upper floors. Counting the victims also continues among the living. Many controllers were devastated beyond their capacity for returning to work. Many of those that have returned still hear the voices of the hijackers and the screams of the crews and passengers. Boston ARTCC air-traffic controller Doug McKay's wife was a passenger on AA11. He returned to the facility moments after AA11crashed—he had just dropped her at the airport.

Administrator Garvey was keenly aware of the suffering, and the mammoth job she was asking from every employee. She testified before the Senate Committee on Governmental affairs on Aviation Security Measures expressing condolences to the families and friends of those lost on September 11, while also trying to reassure a shaken nation. Deputy Director Belger was likewise touched by the losses. During his testimony on September 25 he said, "On behalf of the FAA and its employees, some of whom have suffered their own devastating losses, I would like to extend my sympathies to the many thousands of Americans who were victimized by the terrorists' actions. I assure you that all 48,425 employees of the FAA will continue to work night and day to make the air transportation system safe, secure, and ready to meet the needs of our traveling public. We are committed to meeting the challenges that the tragic events of September 11th present. Our energies are focused on maintaining a safe National Airspace System (NAS)." [1]

In an effort to rally all 48,000 employees of the FAA to the job ahead, Garvey praised them by saying: "Employees are staffing new posts, taking on extra assignments, working harder and longer as well as working around-the clock." She continued, "You are the reason we will be able to get our aviation system running again. We still have a big job ahead of us, but we know that the men and women of the FAA can get it done."[2]

As though to echo her words, many throughout the nation were in fact taking up jobs not normally theirs. Mel Freedman, the acting manager of the New York City Flight Standards District Office (FSDO) during September 11, explained the efforts of the people working at the facility he managed, saying: "The New York FSDO Inspectors along with inspectors from the New York International Field Office (IFO) worked and continue to work 24/7 at the Fresh Kills Land Fill [the destination for most dump trucks loaded at Ground Zero] searching for the recorders and at the New York City emergency command center supplying information to the FBI." He continued, saying that it wasn't just the professional personnel who were involved, but everyone, all the way down to the administrative personnel were taking their turns at the garbage dump. [3]

Transportation Secretary Mineta voiced support to the FAA staffers who were putting in long hours doing jobs often not theirs, making sure that the system worked properly. He said, "I must applaud and recognize the many men and women at the FAA who all responded so magnificently on September 11—and who have been working night and day to restore the aviation system—safely and securely." [4]

Messages of consolation and solidarity poured in from all over the world. At the Flight Standards Command Center, Phyllis Duncan recounted words from an Ecuadorian General. He had originally called the Command Center to facilitate the return of a group of Ecuador's citizens to their country after the ground stop went into effect. As he finished his business, he told her, "Miss Duncan, please accept the condolences of the people of Ecuador. We hurt for you, and we can't imagine what you're going through. This is awful, so awful." [5]

The China Air Show opened on September 19. Beth Keck, the FAA's representative to Beijing was requested by local officials to give a few remarks reflecting on the previous week's events. She considered it an honor to have been asked, saying, "In contrast to the passionate anti-American sentiment I have experienced in the recent past, it is finally heartening to be the object of sympathy instead of disdain. While there are people in China who believe America has gotten what it deserves, everyone in Beijing that I've encountered has been truly sympathetic. This morning after the event, I could barely walk out our apartment building with dry eyes, as all the staff solemnly nodded as I walked by, silently acknowledging the tragedy. Our aviation colleagues, to a person, have made it a point to come up to me and express their concerns. It's been touching." [6] Aviation organizations in other countries feel kinship with their brothers and sisters in the U.S.

regularly, but in the days after the attack many were struck with the size of the country's tragedy and the giant effort facing the U.S. aviation organization. John Crichton, President of NAV CANADA the air-traffic control organization in Canada wrote, "I have just recently returned from the very moving commemorative service on Parliament Hill to honor the victims of the recent terrorist attacks in the United States. I was struck by the size of the crowd, probably up to 50 thousand people. It drove home to me in a very poignant way the depth of kinship and sorrow all Canadians feel for our best friends in America." [7] He continued, "Canadians will stand shoulder to shoulder with Americans throughout this ordeal."

A national day of mourning was designated in Ireland and on September 17, the entire nation came to a halt, closing all businesses. It was the first such day in the history of the country. Thousands stood in line for hours, waiting to sign a book of condolences available at the U.S. Embassy in Dublin.

Other federal workers struggled with the damage of the attack. Members of the Pentagon community went back to work in the undamaged portions of the building. In the mean time, a promise had been made to these people and the public that the crushed walls and broken glass would be repaired before the first anniversary of the attack.

Thousands of tons of broken concrete and twisted rebar were hauled from the site. Timbers were used to stabilize the structure while engineering assessments were completed. Demolition teams worked seven days a week, twenty-four hours a day to move all the crumbled debris from the area, so that new work could begin healing the building. By November 19, 2001, the rehabilitation began with the rebuilding of columns. Specialty windows and the Kevlar wall coverings that proved lifesavers during the attack were replaced in addition to other innovations as a result of the lessons learned in the days following the flight of AA77. FAA Tactical manger Kies saw all of the devastation two months later and was to say what a "God awful thing it was to see." He continued, saying that he felt the nation had been very lucky to have lost a relative few in that crash. His good friend and former FAA manager, Neal Planzer who worked in the Pentagon, had immediately come to mind when he heard of the crash. He heaved a sigh of relief when he learned that Planzer was in Europe on the day of the attack. The day Planzer returned to the United States, he drove to the Command Center to see Kies. They spent several minutes recounting the events and talking about how things used to be and how all of that had changed. The first personnel were moved back into the refurbished outer ring (E ring) of the Pentagon on August

15, 2002. The somber, but determined group tentatively sat down at the desks with ghosts among them.

Weeks after the terrorist events, those employees far removed from the disaster areas worried about their fellow employees working in the proximity of Ground Zero in both New York and Washington. As an act of solidarity, the employees in the Western Pacific Regional headquarters created a large banner showing the American flag and penned hundreds of thoughts, prayers, and well wishes on the standard. The regional administrator from Los Angeles, Bill Withycombe, wrote a note to Arlene Feldman, Eastern Region administrator, explaining their actions. "We felt we should do something in addition to giving blood and donations to charity. We are doing all those things too—but since we are on the other side of the country we felt it was something we needed to do as well. Our hope is that the banner will achieve its purpose by raising your employees' spirits and morale as preparing it has raised ours." [8] Other FAA organizations worked to be able to support charities devoted to the New York, Washington, and Pennsylvania disasters. The Dallas-Ft. Worth Tower/TRACON team, Houston ARTCC, and Fairbanks Automated Flight Service Station all collected money to send to the hard hit areas. Staff from the Cleveland ARTCC and many local organizations raised funds for the Todd M. Beamer Foundation. They did so because "The aircraft [UA93] passed through Cleveland Center's airspace before crashing in Pennsylvania. Todd Beamer was one of the passengers who helped down Flight 93 before it reached its intended target." [9]

Many in the nation supported the people of the FAA in very personal ways that will always be treasured. On November 9 as Norma Lesser, special assistant to the acting associate administrator for Air Traffic Services, was traveling the infamous Washington, D.C. beltway in Maryland, she glanced up and saw a sign that made her heart beat faster. Someone had fashioned a rather quaint sign saying, "God Bless the FAA."

School children sent letters of condolences. Sherwood Heights Elementary School children made posters and wrote letters supporting the country and decided to send them to the FAA as a thank you gesture for what that agency was doing. The recipient, Liz Smiley from the Office of Civil Aviation Security in Washington was touched when she read lines such as the one from Tyler that said, "Americans have courage to fight the darker side. We have liberty every day and night. That is why I am proud to be an American." [10] Another student, John, wrote, "I am proud to be an American because we can bike and play. We have food to eat and we give food to people all over the world even Afghanistan." [11] Smiley was buoyed by the children's sentiments saying, "I was touched. It was completely unexpected. In the midst of all the darkness and the working and everything we were going through, it was this bright shining light. It was a huge morale boost." [12]

Children of FAA employees felt the darker side. NAS Implementation analyst Neil Angelotti wrote his memories of the attacks on the web site *FAA Responds*. He said, "How do I explain the tragic events of 9/11 to a six-year old? That was the most challenging task that I've faced in my parenting career." He struggled. "I tried to explain to my son that the terrorists didn't like the United States and our involvement in other countries. That they didn't even care about their own lives or the lives of others and that's why they crashed the planes. I tried to explain that I would be safe even though I am a government worker and often fly on airplanes because security would be improved." Neil said that this seemed to satisfy his child and thought he had forgotten about it until a few days later when his little boy looked up and said, "There are going to be a lot of funerals." [13]

Mark Miglietta, New York ARTCC staff member remembers as he worked with the Suffolk County SWAT team on securing the control facility, he heard one of the heavily armed policemen on the phone to his young daughter say, "Daddy has a big gun and is safe so don't worry." [14] Michael Shannon who had been at the Shankesville site said, "That day, I saw my children's environment, our nation's environment blatantly threatened and brutalized by militants. My priorities as a father, patriot (National Guardsman), and a federal employee are to continue working to ensure a safe environment for my children, my country, and the flying public!" [15] On and on it went, with all the stress trickling down to the children.

Administrator Garvey continued to empathize with those who worked for her. Her words to each employee in a letter she sent to every person's home emphasized the criticality of their service. "One thing is certain—the events of this past week dramatically underscored the critical importance of aviation—to our nation's economy and to our way of life." She continued, "It stressed for all of us the vital role we in the FAA have in helping make aviation safer and more secure. I know I can count on each one of you as I assure the flying public—as I assure Americans—that the FAA will do whatever is necessary to provide a safe and secure system." [16]

Finally, a bright spot opened in the gloom and fear when Reagan National Airport was allowed to reopen on October 4. President George W. Bush traveled to the vaulted airport terminal to spread the good news that the city's gateway was open for business. But only after heavy lobbying from the FAA, Capitol Hill, and local business did the tide turn. Security measures are still probably more stringent at this airport than any other in the nation—armed air marshals fly on all incoming and outgoing flights at Reagan National Airport and no one is allowed to leave his seat during the thirty minutes after taking off and thirty minutes before landing. New navigation technology, planned before the terrorist attacks, will straighten the upriver approach path, guiding planes by satellite technology, allowing extremely rigorous monitoring of the path of all incoming jets. A stopgap version of the straightened path now takes some of the airplanes over residential sections of the city, subjecting them to additional noise, but it makes flying into and out of the airport much safer for those on the ground.

A very strict curfew, relaxed over the years of quieter jet engines, was reinstated so that at exactly 7:00am planes could begin to take off and only those that had cleared the outer marker by 10:00pm or earlier were allowed to land. Because in the aviation industry minutes equal dollars, words were parsed to the letter with questions arising as to what precisely could happen at 7:00am—was it actually throttle forward and wheels up at that hour or something else? Finally, Deputy Administrator Monte Belger defined the phraseology as meaning that the 7:00am curfew-breaking activity consisted of pushback. No more or no less.

After the reopening, air-traffic control became a nightmare at Reagan National Airport. Significant numbers of general aviation planes had been given waivers to intrude into the airspace surrounding the airport. All of these waivers were on paper, requiring a lengthy coordination with the controller each time a waivered craft wanted to fly through or to the area. The press wanted to fly over the Pentagon, showing the damaged building. Federal helicopters wanted to fly from a nearby heliport. And myriad local law enforcement planes and helicopters required clearance. As each airplane moved through the air, claiming a waiver, the controllers had to hand check the paper waiver to ensure that permission had been granted. Boeing 757 aircraft were banned from utilizing the tarmac out of fear that planes with large fuel capacity flying near the Pentagon and downtown Washington are too great a risk to allow. General aviation flights were not allowed to return either. Runway 15, a short diagonal runway used by commuter propjets was ruled out for landings and its inverse, runway 33, was disallowed for departures. Years of power-adjust rules have been abandoned at the discretion of each pilot, hopefully giving more control to the pilot and making landings safer. Noise near the airport has become considerably more intense and residential complaints have grown as each jet lands and takes off.

The personnel at the FAA raced to accelerate an ongoing program of deploying more security systems in each airport. Technology and funding dilemmas had slowed its original schedule before September 11. On October 11, 2001 Administrator Garvey testified before Congress to the Subcommittee on Aviation on the deployment and use of security equipment, saying that more copies of the Explosive Detection System (EDS) were being installed. The EDS, a van-sized piece of equipment, will be installed at major American airports and used to inspect passenger baggage. Another security system being deployed even before September 11 was the trace-detection system, a machine capable of sniffing minute traces of explosive materials on baggage, both checked and carryon. Acquisition program management staff for each of these programs began working around the clock to buy adequate amounts of both technologies. Installation of one of these systems at every airport used by commercial aircraft (about 450) has been legislated by Congress to occur before the end of November 2002. But in a country containing over ten of the twenty busiest airports in the world, this was not easy. Despite the fact that overtaxing the manufacturing capacity of product companies put the effort in jeopardy, the FAA program personnel and Transportation Security Administration (TSA) staffers worked long hours to ensure that the Congressional mandate was met. Even though the schedule was extraordinarily tight and the entire program became the responsibility of the new TSA organization, the deadline was met in mid-November 2002.

Taking advantage of the power of the Internet, after the attacks, the agency immediately executed a program called *TalkFAA*. Through a web site, fax number, or free phone number, the industry and public were asked to make suggestions of new technology or ideas that might help tighten security in the aviation environment. Tens of thousands of responses have been catalogued and are being reviewed to ensure that the FAA doesn't miss an opportunity to take advantage of an existing or emerging technology or technique for greater aviation security. Administrator Garvey highlighted the call for information in her October 11 Congressional testimony: "Just to make sure that we are not missing anything that is out there, FAA issued an announcement that appears on our web site requesting information about any product or technology that could be helpful in improving aviation security." [17]

The hot line, 1-800-FAA-HELP proved to be a mixed blessing. In many ways it served as a way to connect people with the FAA. Thousands of calls poured in, many of interest, but many were from people reaching out and looking for assurances rather than providing solutions. Often, it seemed, citizens would call the new phone number in order to share their fright. Many times they simply asked for reassurance as to the state of the system. Other calls offered a little comic relief to the hard workers, answering the phones. Some of the suggestions verged on the bizarre. One person called to suggest that all women passengers be required to wear spandex, so that any weapons hidden in their clothing would be immediately noticeable. The caller continued, suggesting that men should not be able to wear belts because of the potential value as a weapon. Another suggested the use of a net suspended from the ceiling of an airplane that could be dropped onto any potential terrorist. A flexible floor was also recommended so that with the push of a button waves could be created causing the bad guy to loose his footing and be vulnerable to capture. One idea came by mail suggesting that every passenger boarding an airplane be given a baseball bat so that no matter what happened, more "good guys" would have bats than "bad guys," so that the good guys would always prevail.

Twenty FAA volunteers spent months answering the phone, fax, and emails, ensuring that every one was acknowledged. "People are stunned we're actually calling them back," said Therese Boyd, the manager of the FAA's telephone operations. She continued explaining why she had volunteered to answer the phone thousands of time each day saying it was, "…to help not just the FAA, but the public as well." [18] "I really didn't know what I was getting into when I volunteered," she said, "but would I do it all over again? Absolutely. This is what it means to me to be a public servant." [19] After Boyd answered the phones for an entire shift, she went home every night to transcribe messages left on voice mail when the personnel were busy.

Washington, D.C. FAA staffer Peggy Gervasi transcribed voice mails for several weeks. She described her stint with the public by saying, "We dealt with some truly wacky security suggestions, confiscated personal items at airports, reports of low flying aircraft, complaints about flight restrictions." She said, "Callers were frightened, angry, and frustrated, but through all those negative emotions the love of country and basic decency still came through." [20]

A wife called to turn in her husband as a suspected terrorist. An elderly couple called about transporting their pets. "They were moving to Hawaii to retire, but a U.S. carrier refused to let them transport their beloved cats, claiming the FAA prohibited it." Boyd arranged for a three-way telephone conference with the airline, explaining that no such regulation existed and sent the couple on their way. Another woman called trying to arrange a seat on an airplane for her dog. When questioned, she admitted only the dog was flying, she was taking the train. "I'm afraid to fly. The dog's not," she said. [21] When a woman called reporting her husband's ownership of several passports with the same birth date and different names hidden in a shoebox full of money, the FAA staff took her seriously and called the FBI. The hotline personnel received a call several days later from the FBI, thanking them for the "very interesting information." The *Ask FAA* operations manager, Mike Packard, felt that the effort was good for the FAA. "We aren't here to pass the buck. We're here to solve the problem." [22] Messages from all mediums poured into the FAA, many from intensely well meaning people. Most were hand-drawn, stick figures showing various scenarios and weaponry, including one so secret that the creator merely sent a non-disclosure statement for FAA personnel to sign before they would be allowed to hear of its technology.

Technical and procedural solutions were also sought from high-tech companies and professional organizations via the same email, fax, and web page venues that the public had been given. Knowing that insiders often can provide extremely useful information, Administrator Garvey beseeched professional organizations such as Airline Owners and Pilots Association (AOPA) to keep the ideas coming. As a result, thousands of solutions were provided by industry professionals and commercial vendors—many of them worthy of consideration by the FAA. Cockpit door hardening methods were provided as well as new weaponry and detection ideas.

The need for bomb-sniffing dogs was critical. Without sufficient numbers of these specially trained canines available from the normal market channels, the FAA has been forced to begin a special breeding operation of its own. With a gift of five Labrador Retriever puppies from the Australian government, the operation began in January 2002, looking toward the day that the FAA would have adequate numbers to patrol the myriad airports. FAA spokeswoman, Rebecca Trexler commented in a *Washington Post* article about the effort, saying they preferred dogs with good energy levels and stamina such as Labradors and Malinois, but she said, "We'd take a pink poodle if he was qualified." [23]

Finally, during the weeks and months after the attack, there began to be time for the small things again. Sleep was allowed to the executives and some of the security personnel, while small passings were once again observed. Attention began to return to that day in the future where capacity would again be an issue at airports and normal things began to make a difference again. Sabra Kaulia, Airspace Management leader, felt normal return when the first routine email was routed to her asking for precision runway monitor system procedures and insight into the plan that would be used in dealing with air-traffic delays in the summer of 2002. People were beginning to look forward and not backward. An FAA publication noted that Clifford the duck, Biorka Island, Alaska, mascot, who thought he was a dog and had regularly accompanied the FAA technicians around like a dog, had been killed by a wild mink. In other words, life went on and struggled toward "normal."

FAA investigator Tony Ferrante says his organization hasn't returned to normal and probably won't for a long time to come. The litigation that is on the horizon concerning all four accidents is like a tidal wave heading for his organization. As of May 2002, they had only completed two accident packages that contain every pertinent detail about the wreck. Two more remain. The Massaoui trial (the man accused of being the twentieth hijacker), still pending, will require an enormous amount of time for preparation as will the prosecution of Richard Reed, the tennis-shoe bomber captured in December 2001. Ferrante estimates that it will take around ten years for the process to grind to completion, leaving his office in a state of higher intensity for that long. These efforts will be background noise to many, but must go on so that the government can be responsive to its citizens.

Eastern Region hasn't returned to "normal" yet, still waiting for the trauma to wear off. Their region contained the sites of all four crashes, and waiting for the next foot to fall is a daily burden. Their motto has become, "Every day is another day away from 9/11, but the next day closer to the next event." Despite the constant watchfulness of these people, they have reason to be proud of what they accomplished. Hatfield says that the actions of many people in the Eastern Region saved lives. He believes more than four planes were destined for hijacking on September 11, but that quick and courageous actions on everyone's part defused the attackers' plans before additional assaults could be carried out. He is also convinced that more attempts will come, a thought echoed by many others in the agency.

Kudos came from unusual sources. The press, not normally a cheerleader for the FAA, assessed the outcome of the ground stop and land-all-planes orders and decided that the agency had done well. None other than the *Washington Post* Transportation Reporter, Don Phillips, said in a March 2002 speech, "Air traffic controllers were among the real heroes of Sept. 11." He continued by saying that all the FAA "got it right" on that day. [24]

10

Rules were added and subtracted after the September 11 attacks almost daily. Jack Kies, FAA Tactical Operations manager, noted that as the situation settled on Tuesday, and the air-traffic control system was completely quiet, rules began to be promulgated. They began as a complex set of categories of inclusion—who could fly into United States' airspace and who couldn't and when. Each industry element—nationally owned and operated commercial airlines, internationally owned and operated airlines, nationally owned freight airlines, internationally owned freight airlines, etc.—was considered and authorized for return to U.S. skies, or not. Certain carriers didn't meet the security requirements and were told to stay home. General aviation planes were considered as well, but their well-being was far down on the priority scale. Determining which flights, by airline and by flight number, became a very time-consuming job for the Command Center as well as the controllers who were in the process of trying to move traffic around the nation.

Often different rules of engagement were being disseminated from different law enforcement agencies. Reagan National Airport proved to be the most difficult location for everyone to agree upon the rules. Finally, a code-word system was implemented, so that controllers could tell if a pilot was in fact a "good guy." Many of the pilots used to simply landing planes did not adhere to the new James Bondian style of terrorist mitigation and failed to give the code. All were denied landing rights at National and ultimately made unscheduled trips to nearby, but more secure Dulles Airport.

Ultimately, it became very important to get as many airplanes into the air as possible, as soon as possible. Huge economic issues rode on the backs of every airline and everyone in the FAA was very aware of the problem. Mother Nature also threw a few wrenches into the works, demanding ultra-close collaboration between the agency and the industry. The planning telcons that had originated from the Command Center to all airlines, regularly held every two hours, continued with a new intensity. Confirmation that the original vision of the creation of the Command Center was right on the mark was proven time and again. Management opinion is that without its centralized response on September 11 and the days after, the entire effort of tactical command of airspace control would have been fractured and far less effective than it was. Tactical Operations manager Kies noted after reviewing the total effort: "All things considered, the FAA and the Command Center had put forth a terrific effort."

Subsequent to September 11, Congress made about $40 billion available to members of the aviation industry. This is for operational support due to the loss of revenue as a result of many fewer passengers, as well as upgrading various security processes and equipment all across the country. Part of this effort, in response to one of the blue-ribbon panels, was to upgrade the cockpit doors on each airliner. The FAA's decision was celebrated in February 2002, according to *USA Today* when recounting the hair-raising story of a Miami-to-Argentina flight where an unruly passenger tried to break into the cockpit. The editorial said that, within weeks of September 11, the "Federal Aviation Administration made rule changes that allowed the airlines to reinforce cockpit doors with steel bars or other barriers, and the airlines quickly responded." The story continued: "Protecting passengers while ensuring pilots can fly the plane is an unbeatable combination. Thanks to some quick action by the FAA, it's one that's well within reach." [1]

The next obvious targets for future terrorists are the freight-only air carriers. The FAA is considering stringent new security rules for this sector of the industry. Even though managers throughout the country, responsible for the bottom lines in each of their respective companies have flinched at the thought of additional security for freight, these potential freight-only missiles will now be subjected to increasing security. These companies, with no passengers aboard, have always been considered less of a hijacking threat and therefore, have been regulated less stringently. Strengthening regulations pertaining to them would probably, "add billions of dollars to the billions already slated for securing passengers." [2] It would also raise the cost of doing business, making it a hard decision for the FAA—once again the regulators are faced with the dichotomy of choosing between safety and the financial well being of the aviation industry.

As a safety precaution, in a move that according to FAA spokeswoman Rebecca Trexler was "unprecedented in our history," the FAA halted cargo shipments on all passenger planes, along with all the other commercial flights immediately after September 11—the ban was lifted on September 16. [3]

Barely had things calmed down until the FAA began looking beyond the horizon, trying to fathom the upcoming security issues they might face. Obviously, the Superbowl and the 2002 Olympics at Salt Lake City, Utah, weighed heavily on their minds. Daily meetings with the Secret Service, Utah Public Safety Command, and U.S. Customs helped define airspace restrictions and other security measures. Exceptional precautions surrounded each of the large gatherings with the commensurate involvement of FAA personnel. A security zone in the air was established with stringent rules for entry into the restricted airspace. The planning and foresight paid off because despite the tension and worry, no security issues arose at either venue.

11

Ultimately, we have to look at our federal agencies and decide they are us. Without them no national effort in homeland defense or rescue would or will ever be possible. The people of the FAA gave their best, some of them almost twenty-four hours a day, for weeks on end, without fuss and expecting nothing more than a paycheck. Which of us would be willing to do that?

In order to ensure that our national services continue at such a high standard, we must all be willing, at a minimum to support those who take up the battle flag on our behalf. Secretary of Transportation Mineta provided perspective in September 25, 2001, remarks to Department of Transportation employees when he said, "I wish I could tell you that your efforts are drawing to a close, but I cannot. Our nation has entered into a new era in the history of transportation, an era in which one of our most cherished freedoms—the basic freedom of mobility—has been challenged." He continued, exhorting the federal employees to "...ensure that all Americans know that this challenge is being met." He left them with a final thought, "But if those who brought down one of America's proudest buildings also believe they can bring down our faith in our transportations systems, we will emphatically prove them wrong." [1]

As Administrator Garvey testified on October 11, 2001, to Congress, outlining the huge job she and other FAA personnel faced. "Because civil aviation exists in a dynamic environment, the FAA must develop a security system that optimizes the strengths of a number of different technologies. This system must be responsive to the means of attack and must be able to anticipate future risk to the civil aviation environment. It is clear that through constant vigilance, the application of new technologies and procedures, and with the help of its national and international partners, that the FAA will succeed in its civil aviation security mission. In a democracy, there is always a balance between freedom and security. Our transportation system, reflecting the value of our society, has always operated in an open and accessible manner, and we are working hard to ensure that they will do so again." [2] But in the long run, all the agencies, administrations, and countless other organizations must not simply endeavor to respond to short-term events. As with all other organizations, it's been noted many times that the FAA's guidance must not be made in response "...to dangers revealed by spectacular disasters. They must be welded into policy that keeps abreast of the industry's growth and rapid technical change. In the regulation of aviation, as in flight itself, momentum is vital." [3]

By 2004, more than half of our federal employees will be eligible to retire, creating a huge void and brain drain at a time we might not be able to afford it. Enticing some of them to stay longer might work in some cases, but in the long run replacement with quality recruits will become a national imperative. Former FAAer Courtney Tucker was one of those who had retired before the terrorists attacked. He had been a member of the Civil Aviation Security Policy and Planning organization of the FAA and was asked to return to duty soon after September 11. He was glad to return, saying, "I first took the oath to protect and defend the Constitution of the United States in September 1963 as a Navy ROTC Midshipman, then as a Marine Officer, and again as an OST [Department of Transportation] and FAA employee. I came back because I was given a second chance to serve my country in its time of need. There is no greater gift, no higher honor in life. This time, I'll do better." [4]

Public confidence in the federal government has always been shaky, but when measured by the Brookings Institution's Presidential Appointee Initiative in July 2001, thirty-six percent of the respondents said they didn't trust the government. Another fifty-six percent noted they trusted the government only a fair amount with only seven percent confessing they trusted the government a great deal. A full seventy percent said they trusted the government to do the right thing only some of the time or not at all. Scary confessions considering this entity touches us in sometimes hidden, but very profound and personal ways each and every day.

In the wake of September 11, the armed-services recruiting centers were deluged with volunteers, the vast majority too old to qualify. Noticeably absent were volunteers of recruitable age. Hope does come to us from other quarters. A *Washington Post* story written on October 22, 2001 noted a shift in some people's ambitions when it profiled Wharton Business School student Kristine Kippins' sudden change in aspirations from becoming a stock broker and making lots of money to aiming at the Peace Corps with an ultimate goal of running for public office. By way of explanation, the author said, "National crises have always drawn people to the national capital, many of them the best and brightest." [5]

Surges in public service have been documented many times, mostly in the context of a national or international crisis. Washington, DC, subsequent to the Civil War, was transformed into a fully-fledged city as it finally came into its own as the federal seat of government and emerging leader of the world. New Deal,

World War II, Great Society, and Viet Nam War surges can be easily documented as well.

Whatever the reason, the need will stretch long past September 11, 2001. The insidious nature of the attack and the attackers will require that we inspire highly intelligent and motivated youngsters to take the place of those fighting the battle today. The federal government will require it and the country will demand it.

Those who say the United States, but mostly Washington and New York City will never be the same, underestimate the strength of this nation and its inhabitants. On any given day, we are never the same from one day to the next, yet we always heal and with the help of each other, be we civilian, military, or federal, we are always better for it.

This nation has faced near-mortal wounds before, but with God-given strength and leadership it survives and thrives. For more than a decade in the early part of the twentieth century, the unemployment rate held steady at over twenty percent. The financial markets collapsed in 1929. Two major wars swept the world and several other smaller conflicts, no less damaging to the country, raged. Yet, despite the beating the nation experienced, we have always managed a comeback, often because of our civil servants who serve as the stabilizing forces of our government.

Pearl Harbor (a violent invasion of our soil) and the assassination of a president (the introduction of violence on a national basis) have played havoc with our national psyche. But inevitably, we have gathered our wits and persevered. We take our lumps and redirect our efforts to a means of fixing the problem—whether it is rebuilding a continent after a world war or creating a technology that would take us to the moon, we've always survived the damage. This is no different.

The launch of Sputnik, the first manmade object ever to orbit the Earth brought some sobering thoughts to our country. Like September 11, the launch came at a time of prosperity throughout the country and caused some serious soul searching. Suddenly, the things we took for granted became precious and we valued our way of life even more in the face of foreign pressure. In a 1957 radio presentation, Gabriel Heatter, news broadcaster for the Mutual Broadcasting System, was grateful for the kick in the pants from the Russians. He said, "You gave us a shock which hit many people as hard as Pearl Harbor. You hit our pride a frightful blow. A nation, like a man, can grow soft and complacent." [6] Now people are saying, once again, that we've had an attack along the lines of Pearl Harbor, affording several generations of Americans who have only known peace and prosperity a new world in which to function. We may have grown complacent in the face of too many material goods, but we've been given a wakeup call and we must do our best to answer it.

Notes

Notes to Chapter 1

1. David S. Broder, "A Crisis in Public Service," *Washington Post* (October 21, 2001): B7—President George W. Bush pronounced civil service as a "noble calling and a public trust." Just over a year later he announced a cut in pay raises for most non-military civil servants.

2. Stephen Barr, "The People to Whom the Public Looks for Help in a Crisis," *Washington Post* (September 16, 2001): C2.

3. David Kerr, "A Trend," *ARA Notes* (December 17, 2001): 2.

4. Stephen Barr, (September 16, 2001): C2.

Notes to Chapter 2

1. Dan Balz and Bob Woodward, "A Presidency Defined in One Speech," *Washington Post* (February 2, 2002): A13.

Notes to Chapter 3

1. David Maraniss, "September 11, 2001," *Washington Post* (September 16, 2001): A24.

2. Ibid.

3. Matthew L. Wald and Kevin Sack, "'We Have Some Planes,' Hijacker Told Controller," *New York Times* (October 15, 2001): A1.

4. "Pattern of Terror Echoes in Plane Data," *Washington Post* (October 17, 2001): A14.

5. Charlie Lane, Don Phillips, and David Snyder, "A Sky Filled With Chaos, Uncertainty and True Heroism," *Washington Post* (September 17, 2001): A3.

6. Ibid.

7. Ibid.

8. David Maraniss (September 16, 2001): A25.

9. Matthew L. Wald and Kevin Sack, (October 15, 2001): A1.

10. Katherine Shaver, "Crowded Skies Prompt FAA to Shuffle Flight Paths, *Washington Post* (April 15, 2002): F1.

11. Matthew L. Wald and Kevin Sack, (October 15, 2001): A1.

12. David Maraniss (September 16, 2001): A25.

13. H. Darr Beiser, "Amid Terror a Drastic Decision: Clear the Skies," *USA Today* (August 12, 2002).

14. Nick Komons, *Bonfires to Beacons; Federal Civil Aviation Policy Under The Air Commerce Act—1926–1938* (Washington, D.C.,:U.S. Department of Transportation—Federal Aviation Administration, 1978), 299.

15. "Pattern of Terror Echoes in Plane Data," *Washington Post* (October 17, 2001): A14.

Notes to Chapter 4

1. Bradley Graham, "Military Alerted Before Attacks," *Washington Post* (September 15, 2001): A18.

2. Dan Balz and Bob Woodward, "America's Chaotic Road to War," *Washington Post* (January 27, 2002): A11.

3. Ibid.

4. H. Darr Beiser, (August 12, 2002).

5. David Bond, "Crisis at Herndon: 11 Airplanes Astray," *Aviation Week & Space Technology* (December 17, 2001): 99.

6. Andrew Alderson and Susan Bisset, "The Extraordinary Last Calls of Flight UA 93, *The Telegraph* (October 21, 2001).

7. Karen Breslau, "The Final Moments of United Flight 93," *Newsweek* (September 25, 2001).

8. John Croft, "Terrorists May Have Planned Double Hits in Washington," *Aviation Week & Space Technology* (September 17, 2001): 44.

Notes to Chapter 5

1. William B. Scott, "F-16 Pilots Considered Ramming Flight 93," *Aviation Week & Space Technology: Aviation Week's AviationNow.com* (September 9, 2002).

2. H. Darr Beiser, (August 12, 2002).

3. Jane Garvey, "Statement of the Honorable Jane F. Garvey before the House Committee on Appropriations Subcommittee on Transportation and Related Agencies Concerning Air Traffic Control Delays and Capacity," (August 2, 2001): 1.

4. Monte Belger, "Acting Deputy Administrator Federal Aviation Administration Before the Senate Committee on Governmental Affairs on Aviation Security Measures Including the Screening of Passengers and Property," (September 25, 2001): 1.

5. Nick Komons, *Bonfires to Beacons:* prologue.

6. John R. M. Wilson, *Turbulence Aloft; The Civil Aeronautics Administration Amid Wars and Rumors of Wars 1938–1953* (U.S. Department of Transportation, Federal Aviation Administration, Washington, D.C., 1979): 10.

7. Nick Komons, *Bonfires to Beacons*: 286.

8. Stuart I. Rochester, *Takeoff at Mid-Century; Federal Civil Aviation Policy in the Eisenhower Years, 1953–1961* (U.S. Department of Transportation—Federal Aviation Administration, Washington, D.C., 1976): 124.

9. John R. M. Wilson, *Turbulence Aloft:* 245.

10. Ibid., p. 255.

11. Stuart I. Rochester, *Takeoff at Mid-Century:* 131.

12. John R. M. Wilson, *Turbulence Aloft:* 28.

13. Stuart I. Rochester, *Takeoff at Mid-Century:* 125.

14. John R. M. Wilson, *Turbulence Aloft:* 209.

15. Richard J. Kent, Jr., *Safe, Separated, and Soaring: A History of Federal Civil Aviation Policy 1961–1972* (U.S. Department of Transportation, Federal Aviation Administration, Washington, D.C., 1980): 4.

16. Jerry Lavey, "The Human Face of the FAA," *AOA Highlights* (November 9, 2001).

17. George Cahlink, "Change is in the Air," *GovExec Magazine* (June 1, 2002): 1.

Notes to Chapter 6

1. Anonymous, "Pushback: Newark Airport, 8:45a.m.," *Air & Space Magazine* (December2001/January 2002): 21.

2. H. Darr Beiser, (August 12, 2002): 1A.

3. Jane Garvey, "Statement of Jane F. Garvey Administrator, Federal Aviation Administration Before the Subcommittee on Aviation, Committee on Transportation and Infrastructure, on Aviation Security Following the Terrorist Attack on September 11," (September 21, 2001): 2.

4. Jane Garvey, "Remarks Prepared for Delivery to the AOPA Expo 2001," (November 8, 2001): 1.

5. David Bond, (December 17, 2001): 96.

6. Ibid., p. 97.

7. Ibid., p. 98.

8. Annette Gowans, email to Jerry Lavey (November 16, 2001).

9. David Bond, (December 17, 2001): 99.

10. Ibid.

11. Annette Gowans, (November 16, 2001).

12. Jerry Lavey, "A Word of Appreciation for the FAA," *AOA Highlights* (September 19, 2001).

13. *freqofnature.com*, "Air-Defense Patrols Used Nuclear-War Procedures," (September 30, 2001).

14. John Croft, (September 17, 2001): 46.

15. Steven King, "9/11 Air Ambulance" *FAA Responds* (September 11, 2002).

16. FAA Press Release, "Airports to Remain Closed, Mineta Says," (September 12, 2001): 1.

17. Ibid., p.2.

18. Edmund Preston, *Troubled Passage: The Federal Aviation Administration During the Nixon-Ford Term, 1973–1977* (U.S. Department of Transportation, Federal Aviation Administration, Washington, D.C. 1987): 39.

Notes to Chapter 7

1. "FAA Historical Chronology, 1926–1996" page for August 10, 1961.

2. "Top-to-Bottom Review of Security Begins," *FAA Intercom* (October 2001): 6.

3. Jerry Lavey, "What's It Like at the FAA These Days?" *AOA Highlights* (October 4, 2001).

4. Lindsey Layton, "A Day of Courage, Patriotism, Anxiety," *Washington Post* (September 13, 2001): B1.

5. Jerry Lavey, "FAAers Going the Extra Mile," *AOA Highlights* (September 27, 2001).

6. John Krepp, "A New York Perspective," *FAA Responds* (September 11, 2002).

7. Jerry Lavey, "FAAers Going the Extra Mile."

8. Jerry Lavey, "Feeding the Hungry, Clothing the Naked," *AOA Highlights* (September 18, 2001).

9. FAA Press Release, "Statement of U.S. Secretary of Transportation Norman Y. Mineta," (September 13, 2001): 1.

10. Jane Garvey, "Remarks Prepared for Delivery at AOPA Expo 2001," (November 8, 2001): 2.

11. Frank Swoboda and Martha McNeil Hamilton, "U.S. Airlines Struggle Back Into Operation," *Washington Post* (September 15, 2001): A16.

12. Michael Shannon, "Ensuring the Future," *FAA Responds* (September 11, 2002).

13. Peter Perl, "Hallowed Ground," *Washington Post Magazine* (May 12, 2002): 44.

14. Craig Timberg and Lindsey Layton, "Officials Push to Reopen National," *Washington Post* (September 15, 2001): A16.

15. "FAA Historical Chronology, 1926–1996" page for October 22, 1962.

16. "FAA Historical Chronology, 1926–1996" page for 1951.

17. Jerry Lavey, "FAAers Standing Tall," *AOA Highlights* (September 21, 2001).

18. Jane Garvey, "Remarks Prepared for Delivery at AOPA Expo 2001," (November 8, 2001): 1.

19. Jerry Lavey, "FAA Eases Flight Restrictions on General Aviations," *AOA Highlights* (December 21, 2001).

20. Amy Goldstein and Mike Allen, "Bush Vows to Defeat Terror, Recession," *Washington Post* (January 30, 2002): A13.

21. Jane Garvey, "Statement of Jane F. Garvey Administrator, Federal Aviation Administration before the Subcommittee on Aviation, Committee on Transportation and Infrastructure, on Aviation Security Following the Terrorist Attack on September 11," (September 21, 2002): 4.

22. Dan Balz and Bob Woodward, "A Presidency Defined in One Speech," *Washington Post* (February 2, 2002): A13.

Notes to Chapter 8

1. Keith L. Alexander, "The View From the Ground," *Washington Post* (December 30, 2001): H6.

2. John R. M. Wilson, *Turbulence Aloft,* 9.

3. Keith L. Alexander, H7.

4. Nick Komons, *Bonfires to Beacons,* forward.

5. Douglas Gillies, "Changes in the Wind," *Annual Report to the NIUSR 2002 Executive Board:* 2.

Notes to Chapter 9

1. Monte Belger, "Acting Deputy Administrator, Federal Aviation Administration Before the Senate Committee on Governmental Affairs on Aviation Security Measures Including the Screening of Passengers and Property," (September 25, 2001): 1.

2. "FAA Mourns Fallen, Prepares for New Era in Commercial Aviation," *FAA Intercom* (October 2001): 1.

3. Jerry Lavey, "Other Duties As Assigned," *AOA Highlights* (September 25, 2001).

4. Jerry Lavey, "Secretary Gives Gold Medal to Controllers," *AOA Highlights* (November 2, 2001).

5. Jerry Lavey, "FAAers Going the Extra Mile," *AOA Highlights* (September 27, 2001).

6. Jerry Lavey, "Report From Beijing," *AOA Highlights* (September 21, 2001).

7. Jerry Lavey, "Canada Feels a Special Sorrow and Kinship," *AOA Highlights* (September 21, 2001).

8.   Jerry Lavey, "West is East and East is West," *AOA Highlights* (October 19, 2001).

9.   "How Do You Spell Relief: F-A-A," *FAA Intercom* (December 2001): 5.

10. "Like American, Butterflies are Free," *FAA Intercom* (December 2001): 16.

11. Ibid.

12. Ibid.

13. Neil Angelotti, "How Do I Explain?" *FAA Responds* (September 11, 2002).

14. Mark Miglietta, "at NY ARTCC" *FAA Responds* (September 11, 2002).

15. Michael Shannon, "Ensuring the Future!" *FAA Responds* (September 11, 2002).

16. "FAA's Vital Role," *FAA Intercom* (October 2001): 7.

17. Jane Garvey, "Statement of Jane F. Garvey, Administrator of the Federal Aviation Administration Before the Committee on Transportation and Infrastructure Subcommittee on Aviation on the Deployment and Use of Security Equipment," (October 11, 2001): 2.

18. "Tell FAA Has Tales to Tell," *FAA Intercom* (January 2002): 8.

19. Therese Boyd, *FAA Responds* (September 11, 2002).

20. Peggy Gervasi, "First and Foremost, We're Americans," *FAA Responds* (September 11, 2002).

21. "The Buck Stops with Tell FAA," *FAA Intercom* (January 2002): 8.

22. Ibid.

23. Jerry Lavey, "FAA's Going to the Dogs," *AOA Highlights* (January 11, 2002).

24. Don Phillips, "Will Aviation Ever Be Fun Again?" Aero Club (March 26, 2002).

Notes to Chapter 10

1. Jerry Lavey, "USA Today Lauds FAA for 'Quick Action' on Cockpit Door," *AOA Highlights* (February 15, 2002).

2. Greg Schneider, "Pilots Urge Tighter Cargo Screening," *Washington Post* (January 30, 2002): A7.

3. Ibid.

Notes to Chapter 11

1. "Heartfelt Gratitude," *FAA Intercom* (October 2001): 7.

2. Jane Garvey, "Statement of Jane F. Garvey, Administrator of the Federal Aviation Administration Before the Committee on Transportation and Infrastructure Subcommittee on Aviation on the Deployment and Use of Security Equipment," (October 11, 2001): 2.

3. Edmund Preston, *Troubled Passage*: 3.

4. Courtney Tucker, "A Second Chance," FAA Responds (September 11, 2002).

5. Neil Irwin and Amy Joyce, "In Pursuit of Idealism," *Washington Post* (October 22, 2001): E1.

6. Paul Dickson, *Sputnik, The Shock of the Century* (Walker & Company, New York, 2001): 223.

Selected Bibliography

1. *Air-Defense Patrols Used Nuclear-War Procedures. Defense Week.* September 30, 2001.

2. Balz, Dan and Bob Woodward. *America's Chaotic Road to War. Washington Post.* January 27, 2002.

3. Balz, Dan and Bob Woodward. *A Presidency Defined in One Speech. Washington Post.* February 2, 2002.

4. Balz, Dan, Bob Woodward, and Jeff Himmelman. *Afghan Campaign's Blueprint Emerges. Washington Post.* January 29, 2002.

5. Balz, Dan and Bob Woodward. *A pivotal Day of Grief and Anger. Washington Post.* January 30, 2002.

6. Bicknell, Larry interview. March 28, 2002.

7. Bond, David. *Aviation Will Come Back Gradually From Stand-Down. Aviation Week & Space Technology.* September 17, 2001.

8. Bond, David. *Crisis at Herndon: 11 Airplanes Astray. Aviation Week & Space Technology.* December 17, 2001.

9. The Brookings Institute. *Atomic Audit: The Costs and Consequences of U.S. Nuclear Weapons Since 1940.*

10. Burr, Stephen. *When Lawmakers Bring Up 'Bureaucrats,' It's Probably Not for Praise, Study Finds: Washington Post.* March 31, 2002.

11. Cahlink, George. *Change is in the Air. GovExec.com.* June 1, 2002.

12. Canoles, David interview. March 22, 2002.

13. Croft, John. *Terrorists May Have Planned Double Hits in Washington. Aviation Week & Space Technology.* September 17, 2001.

14. FAA Historian. *Chronology of the Attacks of September 11, 2001, and Subsequent Events through April 15, 2002.*

15. *FAA Historical Chronology: Civil Aviation and the Federal Government. 1926–1996.* 1998.

16. *FAA Intercom.* December 2001.

17. Ferrante, Anthony "Tony" interview. May 6, 2002.

18. Fulghum, David A. *Pentagon Attack Hits Navy Hard. Aviation Week & Space Technology.* September 17, 2001.

19. Greene, Thomas C. *Did U.S. Air Emergency Procedure Aid Suicide Hijackers?. The Register.* September 17, 2001.

20. Kaulia, Sabra interview. February 15, 2002.

21. Kelly, Ed and Cathy Kelly interview. April 3, 2002.

22. Kent, Jr., Richard J. *Safe, Separated, and Soaring: A History of Federal Civil Aviation Policy 1961–1972.* U.S. Department of Transportation. Federal Aviation Administration. Washington, D.C. 1980.

23. Kerr, David. *A Trend. ARA Notes.* December 17, 2001.

24. Kiss, Kevin interview. April 16, 2002.

25. Komons, Nick. *Bonfires to Beacons; Federal Civil Aviation Policy Under The Air Commerce Act—1926–1938.* U.S. Department of Transportation—Federal Aviation Administration. Washington, D.C. 1978.

26. Lavey, Jerry. *AOA Highlights. FAA's Going to the Dogs.* January 11, 2002.

27. Lavey, Jerry. *AOA Highlights. USA Today Lauds FAA for "Quick Action" on Cockpit Door.* February 15, 2002.

28. Lavey, Jerry. *AOA Highlights. What's it Like at the FAA These Days?.* October 4, 2001.

29. Lavey, Jerry. *AOA Highlights. Other Duties as Assigned.* September 25, 2001.

30. Lavey, Jerry. *AOA Highlights*. *FAAers Standing Tall.* September 21, 2001.

31. Lavey, Jerry. *AOA Highlights*. *West is East and East is West.* October 19, 2001.

32. Lavey, Jerry. *AOA Highlights*. *FAA Eases Flight Restrictions on General Aviation.* December 21, 2001.

33. Lavey, Jerry. *AOA Highlights*. *Secretary Gives Gold Medal to Controllers.* November 2, 2001.

34. Lubore, Dave interview. February 2002.

35. Mello, Tony interview. May 2002.

36. *Otis Air Base. Boston Magazine*, January 2002.

37. Peacock, Bill interview. December 20, 2001.

38. Phillips, Don. *FAA, Air Traffic Controllers at Odds Over Security. Washington Post.* February 22, 2002.

39. Press Release. Department of Transportation, U.S. Transportation Secretary Mineta Announces Rapid Response Teams on Airport, Aircraft Security. September 16, 2001.

40. Preston, Edmund. *Troubled Passage; The Federal Aviation Administration During the Nixon-Ford term, 1973–1977.* U.S. Department of Transportation, Federal Aviation Administration. 1987.

41. Ramirez, Luis interview. February 9, 2002.

42. Rochester, Stuart I. *Takeoff at Mid-Century; Federal Civil Aviation Policy in the Eisenhower Years, 1953–1961.* U.S. Department of Transportation—Federal Aviation Administration. Washington, D.C. 1976.

43. Schuessler, Linda interview. May 2002.

44. Scott, William B. *F-16 Pilots Considered Ramming Flight 93. Aviation Week & Space Technology.* September 9, 2002.

45. Shaver, Katherine. *Crowded Skies Prompt FAA to Shuffle Flight Paths: Washington Post.* April 15, 2002.

46. Warshawsky, Mark J. *Testimony of Deputy Assistant Secretary for Economic Policy, U.S. Treasury before the House Financial Services Subcommittee on Oversight and Investigation.* February 27, 2002.

47. *Washington Post Magazine.* May 12, 2002.

48. Wilson, John R. M. *Turbulence Aloft; The Civil Aeronautics Administration Amid Wars and Rumors of Wars 1938–1953.* U.S. Department of Transportation, Federal Aviation Administration. Washington, D.C. 1979.

49. Woodward, Bob and Dan Balz. *We Will Rally the World. Washington Post.* January 28, 2002.

50. Woodward, Bob and Dan Balz, *At Camp David, Advise and Dissent. Washington Post.* January 31, 2002.

51. Woodward, Bob and Dan Balz, *Combating Terrorism: 'It Starts Today.' Washington Post.* February 1, 2002.

Index

0-595-29738-2